Swords into Plowshares:

Our GI Bill

by
Sar A. Levitan
Joyce K. Zickler

Center for Manpower Policy Studies
The George Washington University

Olympus Publishing Company Salt Lake City, Utah

ISBN 0-913420-09-3 (Cloth)
ISBN 0-913420-10-7 (Paper)

Library of Congress Catalog Card Number: 73-77503

This book was prepared under a grant from the
Ford Foundation.

Contents

LIST OF TABLES

LIST OF CHARTS

They shall beat their swords into plowshares,
and their spears into pruning-hooks . . . .

Isaiah 2:4

Preface

Aid to veterans in the United States dates back to colonial times. Until World War II, the benefits system centered around income support and health care to disabled servicemen, indigent veterans, and their survivors. Outlays for these recipients with special needs were the basis of a separate welfare system for a selected clientele and continue to constitute the bulk of Veterans Administration (VA) expenditures. As a result of the numbers added by World War II, the veteran population over 65 years of age will quadruple by 1995, requiring income support and health care in even larger proportions. Outlays for veterans are therefore likely to remain a major growth industry.

Other forms of veterans assistance developed more recently. Before World War II was over, Congress foresaw a pressing problem in the return to civilian life of the 15.6 million veterans over a relatively short period of time. Responding to the anticipated need, Congress created a comprehensive set of problems to ease the social and economic readjustment of veterans. Coverage under the readjustment legislation, popularly known as the GI Bill of Rights, was universal. Moreover, it differed from earlier veterans programs in that it required no test of need or disability, and benefits would be forthcoming immediately after military service ended. The programs were directed at younger veterans.

The rationale for the readjustment programs was also slightly different. The objective was to assist the economic conversion from wartime to peacetime production as well as to reward veterans who had endured prolonged separation from civilian life. The debt of gratitude owed the veterans was coupled with a belief that national interest required larger numbers of college trained people.

Once the government assumed the responsibility to help veterans readjust to civilian life after World War II, similar efforts were revived after the Korean Conflict and the Vietnam War. Peacetime veterans released during the brief intervening period were included as well. Altogether the nation has spent more than $30 billion for veterans' readjustment benefits since World War II, including $24.6 billion for the 13.5 million who enrolled in education and training programs alone.

This volume is part of a broader study devoted to a survey and assessment of the entire range of programs in aid to veterans. It considers readjustment benefits needed by millions of veterans who have been uprooted by the nation's defense requirements: employment assistance, education and training benefits, rehabilitation, and loan guaranties. The impact of these outlays is measured in the investment made in the futures of the millions of people who are able to participate in the programs. Have these programs succeeded in meeting their goals of helping veterans to recoup social and economic losses entailed by military service? What should be the government's responsibilities to veterans if the nation is blessed with sustained peace? Should these efforts be continued if the nation relies upon an all-volunteer armed force with emphasis on the military as an occupation? Finally, what lessons have been learned from the VA's experience in investing in human resources that might be applied to investments for other needy groups?

Following a brief review of the characteristics of the current Vietnam veterans, the volume examines the various measures designed to help veterans find employment. Many veterans, however, are not ready for employment upon discharge from the service. They either want to continue with their interrupted education or to acquire a skill in preparation for employment. The government offers various types of assistance to help veterans continue with their education and training. The bulk of the assistance has been used by veterans who aspire to a college education.

Some 300,000 Vietnam era veterans — about one of every twenty — have suffered some physical or mental impairment, and more than four of every ten are considered sufficiently disabled to qualify for vocational rehabilitation restricted to veterans whose readjustment requires particular attention. A noteworthy variety of the disabled, though not in the traditional sense, is the drug-dependent veteran who may not have been injured in battle but whose afflictions and problems of readjustment are no less serious than the one injured in the line of duty. Particular efforts are now made to help the drug-afflicted veteran.

The final program considered in this volume is housing assistance offered to veterans. Few Vietnam veterans have taken advantage of this program, but the veterans housing program will become more important to them as they mature and form families.

The conclusions reached on the effectiveness of the programs in aid of veterans are based mainly on each program's popularity. The programs generally involve not only a federal investment but also one by the veteran who uses the benefit. He must undertake a period of education or training, spend time in seeking a job, or commit finances to home ownership. Since almost one-half of all eligible veterans have participated in at least one of the readjustment programs, it would appear that they believe the programs to be helpful to them.

The future of veterans' readjustment benefits is necessarily speculative. Assuming sustained peace, the economic and social losses connected with military service will be reduced significantly. The shape of the proposed volunteer armed force will also necessitate changes in veterans programs. As military service develops into an occupation that can provide servicemen with compensation and fringe benefits competitive with civilian employment, separate readjustment programs for veterans will not be required. Military service will not be a duty to be rewarded by the VA, but a job for which the employer is responsible for compensating his employees.

Finally the VA model of delivering education and training support to ex-servicemen may be useful to a government seeking to make greater contributions to its youth. If subsidized education is to be adopted, just social programming dictates that it should be offered on the basis of need. The VA certification and stipend system, with some refinements, could be applied to those who lack the means to complete their education. The cost of such a universally available subsidy would limit its coverage. No matter to whom it is extended, the VA's highly decentralized delivery of the stipend program, allowing for maximum individual choice, merits attention.

The authors are grateful to William Johnston for his critical and insightful review of the draft, to Don Davis for his research assistance on chapters 3 and 4, and to Barbara Pease for her help in preparing the manuscript. Officials of the Veterans Administration and the U.S. Department of Labor were most generous with their time and cooperation in making available the data upon which this volume is based.

This volume was prepared under a grant from the Ford Foundation to George Washington University's Center for Manpower Policy Studies. In accordance with the Foundation's practice, complete responsibility for the preparation of the volume has been left to the authors.

Sar A. Levitan
Joyce K. Zickler

Chapter 1.

Back to Civilian Life

More than six million veterans were separated from military service during the first eight years of the Vietnam era starting on August 4, 1964. Almost two million of these veterans returned to civilian life in fiscal years 1970 and 1971, and an additional three-quarters of a million more during the succeeding year. Less than 2 percent of these veterans were women. Approximately 40 percent have seen duty in Vietnam. Medical and other technological advances have kept alive many injured servicemen who would have perished in previous wars, leaving 308,800 veterans with service-connected disabilities by mid-1972. These included 7.4 percent totally disabled, most of them permanently.

THE PROBLEMS THEY FACE

All of these veterans are subject to the usual aspirations, anxieties, and needs of young adults, but many also have particular problems resulting from their recent military service and their reentry into civilian life. Though many have not experienced difficulty in making the transition to work, education, or some other endeavor, other veterans have

11

faced adjustment problems frequently directly or indirectly relating to their stint of service.

These veterans have reentered civilian society after an average of 2.8 years in the military. Many came directly from combat areas. All have undergone an interruption in their normal lives, leaving jobs or schools to enter military service. For some, the opportunity to work or to continue school was disrupted even before entry into the Armed Forces because they knew that military service was inevitable.

Upon returning, the veteran frequently bore the brunt of societal ambivalence toward the war and toward the men who fought in Vietnam. In a special report on the employment problems of the Vietnam veterans, the National Advisory Council on Vocational Education expressed the country's mood:

> Once again the veterans return from war. The situation is not novel in our history, yet somehow these veterans seem different. They do not return to triumphant parades as in the past, nor do they want them. . . . They do not fit the image of returning heroes. . . . The unpopularity of the war places an additional burden upon the returning veteran. The young veteran finds himself referred to in print and in conversation as a dope addict or trained killer. Often his own peer group tells him what a fool he was to go to Vietnam in the first place. In his absence they have moved ahead in their life pursuits . . . while the veteran . . . must start from the beginning as though his military service made no difference.[1]

The declining support for the Vietnam War created a less than supportive atmosphere for some veterans. In many cases these young men have returned isolated, and to some degree alienated from their peer groups and society at large. The result has been the need for them to make psychological and social adjustments in addition to the other adjustments they had to face in civilian life.

Drug addiction was a major problem, though it is not exclusively a veteran phenomenon. Donald Johnson, Veterans' Affairs Administrator, has estimated that in 1972 about 60,000 veterans were addicts.[2] In addition, there were other health problems — minor and major,

[1] National Advisory Council on Vocational Education, *Employment Problems of the Vietnam Veteran* (Washington, D.C.: National Advisory Council on Vocational Education, February 1, 1972), pp. 1, 3.

[2] Mary Russell, "Drug Therapy Aid for Vets Expanded," *The Washington Post* (June 15, 1972).

physical and mental — attributable to service hardships and conditions for which the veteran needed treatment.

Another critical problem for many veterans was employment (Chart 1). The decline in the Vietnam commitment and accompanying reduction in the size of the Armed Forces has coincided with an economic recession. At a time when the Vietnam era veteran returned to society in the greatest numbers, the nation has witnessed its highest unemployment rates in recent years. It was not until 1972 when the economy began to recover that the unemployment situation for veterans began to improve. The added dimension of the often unsuccessful job hunt became another burden for the veteran to bear. Because more veterans

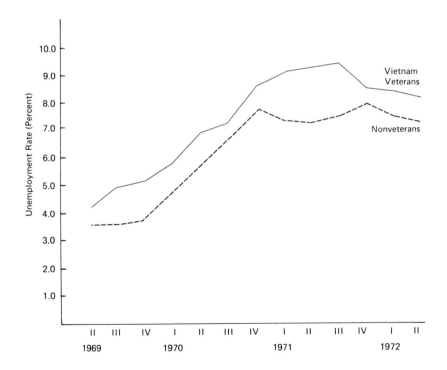

Note: Seasonally adjusted data for 20- to 29-year-old men only.

Source: Bureau of Labor Statistics, U.S. Department of Labor, *Employment and Earnings* (Washington, D.C.: U.S. Government Printing Office, April and July 1972), pp. 137 and 134, respectively.

CHART 1. Unemployment Rates of Veterans and Nonveterans, 1969–72 than nonveterans are reentrants or new entrants into the labor market, higher rates of unemployment are not an unexpected problem. However, the availability of readjustment benefits may modify the veterans' reentry into the labor market. Help is available from many public and private sources to assist the veteran in conducting his job search, returning to school or training, or collecting unemployment compensation benefits. Educational benefits may delay a recently separated veteran's reentry into the labor market, and the availability of unemployment compensation may affect his selection of a job. Nonveterans looking for work may not have such a wide range of choices.

THE VIETNAM VETERAN

More than three of every four Vietnam veterans in 1972 were still in their twenties. While the average age of the total Vietnam veteran population was 27.6 years, the average age of separatees between 1965 and 1972 was 23.[3] Because they were young, the veterans shared the problems that plagued all youth in our nation — those of defining ideals and goals, of assuming responsibilities, and more importantly for their purposes, of obtaining further education or training while facing extremely high levels of unemployment.

The veteran's education or training may have been either directly or indirectly curbed because of military service. However, the young veteran was better educated than his predecessors of World War II or Korea. Fewer Vietnam veterans failed to finish their elementary education, and more went on to complete high school. Only 45 percent of World War II veterans had attained at least a high school education upon leaving the military, compared to 80 percent of Vietnam veterans. The Vietnam veteran had no more college education, however, than his counterparts in earlier wars. In fact, he was slightly less likely to have earned a college diploma because he was younger at the time of his entrance into the military.[4]

The educational attainment of Vietnam veterans also varied significantly from the nonveterans in the same age group (Chart 2). Relatively few veterans had gone to college, compared with their nonveteran counterparts. However, more had completed high school than non-

---

[3] Reports and Statistics Service, Veterans Administration, *Data on Vietnam Era Veterans* (June 1972), p. 19.

[4] *Data on Vietnam Era Veterans*, p. 7.

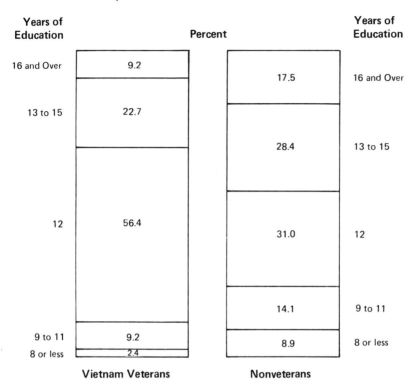

Source: Elizabeth Waldman and Kathryn R. Gover, "Employment Situation of Vietnam Era Veterans," *Monthly Labor Review* (September 1971), p. 10.

CHART 2. Educational Attainment of Vietnam Veterans
and Nonveterans Age 20 to 29 in 1971

veterans. Two major reasons account for the differences in educational level of veterans and others in the same age bracket. First, youths who entered college obtained deferments for continued education, and those who failed to finish high school — concentrated heavily among the poor — were most likely to fail either the mental or physical tests for entry into military service. Thus the veterans were underrepresented in both the higher and lower educational levels. Another factor which contributed to the high percentage of high school graduates among veterans was the opportunity to complete high school equivalency courses while in the service.

Many veterans probably postponed marriage until they finished their military service. Of the enlisted personnel separating from the

military during 1970, 31 percent were married soldiers, compared with
more than half of all the young Vietnam veterans (20 to 24 years of age)
in civilian life.[5] The resulting family responsibilities augmented each
man's readjustment difficulties. Certainly, this affected his decisions as
he examined his priorities and the opportunities available to him.

The racial composition of Vietnam veterans was slightly different
from that of civilians who did not serve. There was a smaller proportion
of minority veterans than minority nonveterans among men 20 to 29
years of age — 9.1 and 12.9 percent, respectively. This disparity is
largely attributable to two factors: higher reenlistment rates for black
servicemen and a higher percentage of blacks failing to meet the physical and mental requirements to enter the military.[6] Minority veterans
were subject to additional social and economic disadvantages accentuat-
ing their other transitional problems (Chart 3).

Work and Training Experience

The average age (23) of the veteran separatees is an age at which,
had it not been for the war, many of the veterans would have finished
college and begun their first job — many of their nonveteran peers had
already accomplished this. Others among the nonveterans had completed some post-high school training and may have been progressing
in a skilled occupation for a year or so. Still others had been employed
throughout this period and had gained valuable work experience and
were now beginning to move up the occupational or income ladder. This
is not true of the returning Vietnam veteran.

Due to his youth, the Vietnam veteran has had little preservice work
experience. Although information about his experience is limited,
former Assistant Secretary of Labor Malcolm Lovell, in testimony[7]

---

[5] Eli S. Flyer, "Profile of DOD First-Term Enlisted Personnel Separating from
Active Duty during 1970," in "Manpower Research Note" (Washington, D.C.:
Office of the Assistant Secretary of Defense, October 1971), Table I (mimeo-
graphed); Elizabeth Waldman, "Viet Nam War Veterans: Transition to Civilian
Life," *Monthly Labor Review* (November 1970), p. 29.

[6] U.S. Bureau of the Census, "The Social and Economic Status of Negroes in
the United States, 1970," *Current Population Reports* (Washington, D.C.: U.S.
Government Printing Office, July 1971), series P-23, no. 38, p. 137, and *Statistical
Abstract of the United States, 1971* (Washington, D.C.: U.S. Government Printing
Office, 1971), p. 241.

[7] Senate Subcommittee on Veterans' Affairs, Committee on Labor and Public
Welfare, 92d Cong., 2d Sess., "Hearings on Unemployment and Overall Readjust-
ment Problems of Returning Veterans" (December 3, 1970) (Washington, D.C.:
U.S. Government Printing Office, 1971), p. 159.

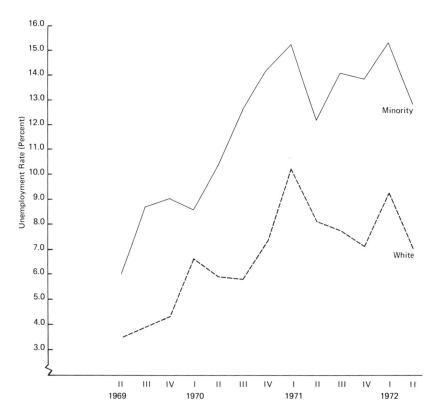

Note: Seasonally unadjusted data for 20- to 29-year-old men only.
Source: Bureau of Labor Statistics, U.S. Department of Labor, *Employment and Earnings* (Washington, D.C.: U.S. Government Printing Office, April and July 1972), pp. 134 and 131, respectively.

CHART 3. Minority Veterans Faced Unemployment Rates
More Than 50 Percent Greater Than White Veterans

before the Senate Committee on Labor and Public Welfare, estimated that at least 350,000, or one-third of the 1970 separatees from military service, were employed before entering military service. Whatever the exact figures, any preservice work experience they may have had was probably in either unskilled or semiskilled occupations — due to the youth and relative lack of education of most men entering the service.

Veterans with little valuable preservice work experience and limited formal education were not generally offered salable skills or education while in the military. A Harris survey[8] in August 1971 found that 44 percent of returning veterans stated that they received no occupational training while in the military. Of those who served between six months and two years, this percentage rose to 58. Moreover, there is a definite relationship between the branch of service and occupational training received. Seven of every 10 Navy and Air Force veterans responded that they had acquired skills training, while less than half of Army and Marine veterans felt that they had been taught a skill.

While acquiring a skill in the military was difficult, transferring that skill to a civilian job was more frustrating for the veteran. In the Harris survey, of the 56 percent who stated they received occupational training in the military, more than half felt that the training was only slightly useful or not useful at all. Employers who hired veterans rated military experience somewhat higher. Three of five employers surveyed felt that military experience was helpful to the veteran.

Another study[9] found that technical skills acquired in the Air Force were transferable to civilian life. Veterans who attained such skills enjoyed higher incomes, greater job satisfaction, and consequently retained positive reactions to military training. But a similar investigation[10] of Army and Navy training disclosed that military experience did little to raise the future income of veterans, especially those assigned to combat and other nontechnical specialties. The Vietnam veterans who were in combat-related military occupations or in service and supply handling, for example, received little or no skills training transferable to civilian life. Often veterans assigned during their military career to jobs requiring technical or craft tasks found that training was either inadequate or too specialized to be adaptable to civilian occupations. Other veterans either could not or did not desire to enter occupational fields for which they were trained in the military.

---

8 Louis Harris and Associates, Inc., *A Study of the Problems Facing Vietnam Era Veterans on Their Readjustment to Civilian Life* (Washington, D.C.: U.S. Government Printing Office, 1972), printed for the use of the Senate Committee on Veterans' Affairs, 92d Cong., 2d Sess., pp. 80–85.

9 Robert B. Richardson, *An Examination of the Transferability of Certain Military Skills and Experience to Civilian Occupations, Final Report* (September 1967), prepared for the Office of Manpower Policy, Evaluation and Research, U.S. Department of Labor, pp. 16–17.

10 Paul A. Weinstein, *Labor Market Activity of Veterans: Some Aspects of Military Spillover, Final Report* (August 1969), prepared for the Office of Education, U.S. Department of Health, Education and Welfare, pp. 13–14.

However, closer examination of the post-service experience of veterans reveals other factors more significant to the veteran's success. Richardson[11] found that formal education was a clearly significant element in the transferability process. Since the military generally selects servicemen for training according to mental aptitude tests and previous education, the problem is compounded. Those with the greatest need for skills training were the least often selected for this training and more often ended up in military occupations which are least transferable to civilian occupations. Weinstein,[12] too, found that among Army and Navy veterans, preservice education and experience was important. Men who previously held civilian jobs related to their military occupational specialty were more successful in transferring their skills back to civilian jobs. For other men, preservice education was an important determinant of post-military success in the labor market.

More than one-third of the men who separated from the service during 1970 were in combat-related or service occupational specialties (Chart 4). For blacks, the proportion was one-half. These men were unable to transfer their military experience to civilian jobs. For them, possible preservice experience was most likely limited. Thus readjustment benefits offered to veterans are of added importance as they reenter civilian life.

Despite the problems veterans experience in readjusting to the civilian labor market, after they were reabsorbed their earnings exceeded that of their nonveteran counterparts (Table 1). In 1970, young veterans (20 to 24 years of age) employed full time earned over $800 more than young nonveterans. The difference in the earnings of older (25 to 29 years of age) veterans and nonveterans who worked full time was less than $100 annually. Veterans who did not work during the year had incomes about six times greater than comparable nonveterans. This occurred because the veterans' reported incomes were inflated with military pay and veterans' benefits.

The "typical" Vietnam veteran in 1972 was a 27.6-year-old high school graduate. When he left the military he was 23 years old. He reentered society much as he had left it, except that he was a few years older and had missed whatever opportunities were available to those

---

11 Robert B. Richardson, *Examination of Transferability, op. cit.*, p. 16.
12 Paul A. Weinstein, *Labor Market Activity of Veterans, op. cit.*, pp. 143–44.

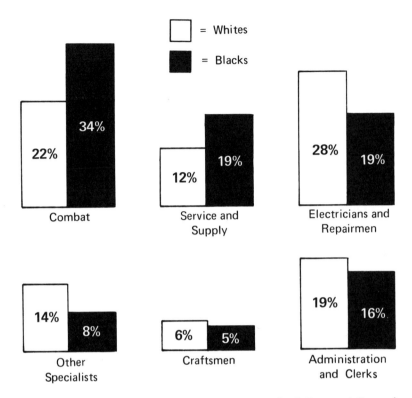

Source: Eli S. Flyer, "Profile of DOD First-Term Enlisted Personnel Separating from Active Service during 1970," in "Manpower Research Note" (Washington, D.C.: Office of the Assistant Secretary of Defense, October 1971), Table II (mimeographed).

CHART 4. One-Half of the Blacks and One-Third of the Whites Separating from the Armed Services in 1970 Were in Military Occupations Not Readily Transferable to Civilian Life

who remained in the United States. But many picked up obstacles in the way of their readjustment. Some were disabled and many had other health problems; some were drug addicts; some were alienated and many were unemployed. And like other young blacks, Chicanos, and American Indians, minority veterans found that discrimination continued to be a barrier to opportunities in civilian life.

THE READJUSTMENT KIT

Upon their return to civilian life, veterans must compete with their peers who have had opportunities to progress in their education, train-

TABLE 1

In 1970, Veterans Had Higher Incomes Than Nonveterans
with Similar Work Experience

	Veterans		Nonveterans	
Work Experience (men only)	Percentage of Work Force	Median Personal Income	Percentage of Work Force	Median Personal Income
Twenty to 24 years:	100%	$4,438	100%	$3,334
Full time	41	7,270	42	6,402
Part time	43	3,747	48	2,087
Did not work	16	2,741	9	a
Twenty-five to 29 years:	100	7,634	100	7,625
Full time	67	8,635	72	8,525
Part time	29	5,350	24	$5,188
Did not work	4%	$3,353	4%	a

a Less than $500.

Source: Elizabeth Waldman and Kathryn R. Gover, "Employment Situation of Vietnam Era Veterans," *Monthly Labor Review* (September 1971), p. 8.

ing, or work. Some veterans may have already finished their formal education in military classrooms or before they entered the service. Others may need further education or training to advance in their career plan. Although the process of informing servicemen of their post-service options for employment and education begins while they are still in the military, some may need encouragement and direction when they return to civilian life. Counseling, then, is the first step in the veteran's readjustment. An evaluation of the individual's goals and needs with the help of a counselor leads the veteran into choosing among the direct routes to jobs and the various education and training programs in which he can enroll. The veteran's options are not dissimilar from his nonveteran peers. However, the readjustment benefits available for veterans may influence his decisions.

The forms of assistance offered to the veteran are varied. Even before their discharge from the military service, some servicemen were offered counseling and training. Upon discharge, according to the law, the veteran is to be placed by his former employer in his preservice job.

Moreover, federal and most state and local governments offer preference to veterans applying for jobs. For the veteran who cannot find a job, the government provides a cushion in the form of unemployment benefits. Finally, the government offers assistance to veterans who opt for added education and training. Disabled veterans receive special consideration in most all readjustment programs.

Approximately $2.5 billion was spent during fiscal year 1972 on education and vocational rehabilitation, unemployment compensation, and housing loans for veterans. Several hundred million more dollars were spent for public employment, manpower training, and employment assistance for veterans who received preference in programs generally available to the public. No precise estimate of the latter expenditures is available, however, since appropriations for such programs do not earmark funds for veterans.

Chapter 2.

Transition to Civilian Employment

Readjustment assistance to the prospective veteran starts in the Armed Forces. Since 1967 the military has operated a modest program to counsel and train servicemen before their return to civilian life. The program, dubbed "Project Transition," focused initially on the vocational training needs of unskilled and deficiently educated military personnel. Since then, Project Transition has expanded to include counseling efforts to help all those who want assistance in finding a civilian job. Moreover, the President's Veterans Program, announced in June 1971, urged that the military not only expand the stateside programs, but also find more ways to provide services to those stationed in Europe and Asia.

Project Transition

The vocational training offered under Project Transition is sponsored by private industry directly, by the U.S. Department of Labor's Manpower Development and Training Act (MDTA) funds, and by other government agencies, including the military. The Armed Forces educational programs are not formally part of Project Transition but remain options to which some men may be referred. Formal training for industry covers a variety of automotive and repairman occupations, as well as sales and computer-related jobs. MDTA training includes many of the same occupations but also provides courses offered by the building trades, unions, and the International Association of Chiefs of Police. MDTA national contracts require that some job placement assistance be given to the men. The United States Armed Forces Institute (USAFI) offers some vocational training through correspondence courses and contracts with schools to offer vocational and technical courses to servicemen. Some 200,000 servicemen received training under Project Transition during its first five years, including 65,000 in fiscal year 1972. They were trained at more than 200 military installations in the United States.

The costs of Project Transition training are generally borne by the sponsors of the classes, not the military itself. Forty percent of the training is offered by private industry. Another 40 percent is financed by Labor Department funds at an estimated cost of $10 million in fiscal year 1972.[1] The U.S. Department of Defense bears only a small portion of the direct costs of Project Transition training in military classrooms, although it incurs the indirect costs of releasing men from active duty and allows the use of military facilities for some programs. Most of the Defense Department's Project Transition budget of $13 million in 1972 was spent on counseling activities.

Men with less than a high school education are encouraged to take the USAFI general education development (GED) tests to obtain a certificate for an eighth grade education or a high school diploma. The Defense Department estimates that 82,000 men successfully completed the high school GED examination during fiscal year 1972. In addition, the 1970 amendments to the GI Bill provided for a predischarge education program (PREP) for deficiently educated servicemen with at least 180 days of active duty. PREP programs are conducted by colleges with VA funds and in cooperation with the military. These courses concentrate on improving the basic reading and mathematics skills to bring disadvantaged servicemen up to the level of high school graduates.

---

[1] U.S. Department of Defense, "Transition Program" (March 20, 1972) (mimeographed), pp. 2–3.

The 1972 Vietnam Era Veterans' Readjustment Assistance Act[2] urged the military and the Veterans Administration to expand PREP courses, particularly overseas, and legislated changes to facilitate participation by servicemen. For example, the required hours were reduced from 25 to 12 per week, half of which time may be taken from active duty.

Although skills training was originally its major goal, perhaps its most significant contribution to veterans' readjustment has become the counseling programs which stimulate interest among the soldiers to use opportunities available for education and employment assistance after discharge. The skills training and career planning needed by young servicemen require more time, resources, and individual attention than the military is able to provide.

The Project Transition program has been plagued by several inherent problems as well as a few unforeseen difficulties. First, the size and worldwide distribution of military installations mean that although counseling is available at each base, training opportunities vary. Many may take whatever course is offered whether or not they intend to use the training in civilian life. Also lack of command support, despite directives from the Pentagon, is apparently a barrier to successful programs at some bases.

Because skills training in the combat areas of Vietnam was obviously impracticable, the military established skills training centers in the United States for men returning from combat duty. By the end of 1972, more than 9,000 men had been trained at the 23 Skills Centers established on military bases.

Not only arranging the training, but the nature of the training itself may cause problems. Still carrying military responsibilities, most enrollees receive only part-time training for 240 hours. Although in some courses — such as police training and automotive skills, sponsored by the Ford Motor Company and General Motors — the 240 hours is an acceptable credential, doubt remains as to whether such limited formal training is readily acceptable to civilian employers. A vocational training program in drafting or electronics at a civilian institute, for example, consists of more than 2,000 hours of training.[3] MDTA institutional

---

2 VIETNAM ERA VETERANS' READJUSTMENT ASSISTANCE ACT OF 1972 (October 24, 1972), Public Law 92-540, §§ 308 and 316(2).

3 House Subcommittee on Education and Training, Committee on Veterans' Affairs, 92d Cong., 1st Sess., "Hearings on Education and Training Programs Admin-

courses normally consist of five or six months (or more than 800 hours) of classwork. Because little follow-up information has been collected, neither the military nor the Labor Department is certain about the success of the Project Transition program.

Developing job opportunities for those men in the vocational programs is also quite difficult when so many men leave the area after training. National contractors (such as the United Brotherhood of Carpenters and Joiners), government agencies (such as the United States Postal Service), and major private companies gain one possible advantage, however, from the geographic mobility of the men. They are able to train a variety of men at a central location without having to absorb all the graduates into a single labor market.

The economic recession and the military's early release policy are among the unpredictable problems which affected Project Transition. The recession of the economy may possibly have affected the program more than other training programs, since private companies can get all the help they need in a slack labor market without investing their own resources in the training of potential workers. The difficulties of Project Transition were compounded by the reduction in military forces in 1971 and 1972, resulting in the early release of many servicemen. Men returning from Vietnam, for whom the Skills Centers were intended, were generally discharged immediately upon their return to the United States and therefore did not benefit from vocational training under Project Transition.

Reaching Out to Veterans

Once the serviceman leaves the Armed Forces, the major governmental responsibility for his readjustment to civilian life rests with the Veterans Administration. Traditionally the VA kept an open-door policy and largely limited its services to veterans who came knocking at the agency's doors. The veteran, either by himself or through the auspices of one of the service organizations, found his way to the VA offices. This situation was particularly true for the nondisabled veteran who might seek education or training benefits.

After the Veterans Readjustment Act of 1966 was passed, however, Vietnam veterans did not use the benefits to the extent anticipated

istered by the Veterans Administration" (November 30, 1971) (Washington, D.C.: U.S. Government Printing Office, 1972), pp. 1733–34.

(based on the experience of earlier programs). To overcome the reluctance of Vietnam veterans to apply for readjustment benefits, the VA initiated Operation Outreach in 1968. This effort extended the responsibilities of the contact division of the VA, who are responsible for the first contact with the veteran. Major efforts have been made to increase the veterans' awareness of benefits and to induce them to apply for VA assistance. VA counseling, budgeted at $7.5 million during 1972, depends heavily upon education and training benefits as a source of readjustment for the veterans.[4]

The Defense Department cooperated with the Veterans Administration's outreach efforts with the dissemination of information in Vietnam combat zones. Experienced VA contact men were assigned to different locations in Vietnam and other areas where troops were stationed. Group orientation was normally the procedure followed, but individual assistance was also available to veterans who desired it. Another form of outreach was a bedside assistance program which attempted to inform servicemen or veterans in hospitals about their benefits and to aid them in initial applications. The VA stationed its contact representatives in more than 180 military hospitals as well as in all veterans hospitals. The VA has also made contact personnel and counselors available at various separation centers in the United States for servicemen. These services were provided at more than 300 separation points, from an "on call" basis when needed to a seven days a week operation at some of the large West Coast centers processing servicemen returning from Vietnam. The Defense Department supplied the VA with a copy of the release papers of each person leaving the service, including educational and other relevant information. A special letter, tailored to the educational circumstances of the veteran, was then sent to each veteran. The letter informed the veteran of the educational and training benefits available, pointed out those most suitable for him, and encouraged him to call and speak personally with the VA representative. Six months after the initial letter was sent, a second letter was mailed.

The VA went to considerable lengths to make the response as painless as possible by installing a toll-free telephone system in 59 larger cities and in six states. If the veteran did not respond to the first letter, two

---

[4] Kenneth B. Hoyt, "Career Education and Career Choice: Implications for the VA" (February 8, 1972), address to the National Task Force on Education and the Vietnam Era Veteran, Veterans Administration, p. 10.

additional follow-up efforts were made over a period of several months. The veteran is dropped from the list of those being actively solicited after no response is made to these three letters, plus possible attempts at telephone contact. The VA officials consider their outreach efforts extremely successful. More than a third of the veterans receiving letters responded, and 47 percent of these requested a return telephone call for further assistance.[5]

Another recent addition to the arsenal of services and facilities available to the veteran are the U.S. veterans assistance centers established to smooth the delivery of services to the recently separated veteran by bringing together a range of services he might need into a one-stop center. The need for a one-stop center was particularly evident in the major urban areas with heavy concentrations of veterans. A network of 72 centers has been established since 1968, mostly as part of the 57 VA regional offices. Representatives from various other agencies were also located in the centers to augment the services provided by the VA. Some areas, such as Los Angeles and Washington, D.C., had separate centers located in areas where minority groups are heavily concentrated.

The United States Civil Service Commission and the U.S. Employment Service were represented in the centers, and contact was maintained with community action groups, housing authorities, the National Urban League, and others. Social workers were added to the staffs in 1969 to offer further assistance in helping the veteran with his various problems. Special efforts were made by center personnel to help veterans without a high school education.

The VA may well have the most extensive operation to reach its potential clientele of any government agency. Not only did the agency have a captive audience in the initial outreach activities in the separation points and the hospitals, it also persisted to reach veterans in their homes. For example, in Texas the VA sent mobile vans staffed with counselors, a social worker, and a state employment interviewer to the rural areas in an attempt to reach disadvantaged veterans who have never seen the inside of a VA office. Other government agencies complemented the VA efforts. To help bring VA services to low-income veterans, the Office of Economic Opportunity funded outreach operations in a dozen

---

[5] Veterans Administration, *Two Years of Outreach, 1968–1970* (Washington, D.C.: U.S. Government Printing Office, 1970), p. 4.

cities. The Appalachian Regional Commission and the Urban Coalition were also involved.[6] The veterans apparently welcomed this attention. According to the Harris survey,[7] more than 60 percent of the veterans interviewed said they appreciated being contacted. Furthermore, two-thirds of the men felt that the VA could be visited conveniently.

Although it is impossible to determine the extent of a veteran's awareness or knowledge of his benefits or the impact of the outreach program in increasing his information, the effect appears sizable. Certainly the attempts have been and continue to be prodigious and the contacts frequent. Whatever the reasons, the participation in the programs has been increasing quite rapidly, particularly in the education and training program. For those who have not chosen to use their benefits, there are continuing efforts to inform them of their alternatives, to encourage them to participate, and to overcome any other impediments that deter them from readjusting successfully.

UNEMPLOYMENT COMPENSATION

In addition to the various services, income support has been an integral part of the veterans' readjustment kit since World War II. Upon leaving the military, veterans of World War II and the Korean Conflict were given a "mustering out pay" of $300 if they had served more than 60 days and had spent some part of their duty outside the Continental United States. Those who only served inside the country were given $200, and those who spent less than 60 days in the Armed Forces were given $100. This severance pay was available to all enlisted men and officers below the rank of major or lieutenant commander.[8] As of July 1, 1966, "mustering out pay" was repealed by Congress. Thus most Vietnam veterans can collect their accrued leave payment as they leave the service, although six states provide "bonus payments" from $100 to $300 to their residents when they return from duty.

Unemployment compensation for veterans was first included in the Veterans Readjustment Act of 1944. Of the 16.1 million World War II

---

[6] Don D. Wright, "Vietnam Veterans: Odd Men Out Move Back in Seattle," *Opportunity* (July 1972), pp. 5–9.

[7] Louis Harris and Associates, Inc., *A Study of the Problems Facing Vietnam Era Veterans on Their Readjustment to Civilian Life* (Washington, D.C.: U.S. Government Printing Office, 1972), printed for the use of the Senate Committee on Veterans' Affairs. 92d Cong., 2d Sess., pp. 226–34.

[8] "Veterans," *Congress and the Nation, 1945–1964* (Washington, D.C.: Congressional Quarterly, Inc., 1965), pp. 1339, 1348.

veterans, 59 percent collected unemployment benefits and joined the "52-20 Club," named for the provision in the law which provided for a maximum of 52 weeks of compensation at $20 per week. The income support served as a cushion to a majority of veterans. Some $4 billion was spent by the federal government between the signing of the bill on June 22, 1944, and July 25, 1949, when the operations ended.

The 1952 Korean GI Bill (Veterans Readjustment Assistance Act of 1952) and later amendments again provided for unemployment benefits for those men who served after June 26, 1950. The maximum length of benefits was reduced to 26 weeks, and the amount that could be collected was raised to $26 per week. Responsibility for administration of the program was delegated to the state unemployment insurance agencies. During the 9.5-year period that the law remained in effect, 1.3 million Korean veterans, or 19 percent of those who served during that conflict, collected $454 million in benefits.

The Ex-Servicemen's Unemployment Compensation Act of 1958 established a permanent system of unemployment insurance, including for the first time all peacetime veterans. Veterans are eligible for unemployment compensation payments within one year after they are honorably discharged, following at least 90 days of active military service. The time requirement can be waived for those discharged because of a service-connected disability. Until 1970 veterans were ineligible to collect unemployment benefits until their accrued leave had expired. While they can register in most states immediately upon their release from active duty, some states postpone benefits if a claimant was paid for accrued leave.[9]

In establishing his claim, the veteran is subject to the laws of the state in which he files. For the most part, a veteran can choose the state in which he wants to file, so long as he has an address established in that state. After initiating his claim, he can move to another state and collect his benefits under the interstate claims system. He thus has an advantage in being able to choose a state where he will collect a higher payment. Maximum payments for unemployment insurance (excluding dependents' allowances) varied in 1972 from $45 a week in Indiana to $105 a week in the District of Columbia.

---

[9] *Manpower Report of the President, 1972* (Washington, D.C.: U.S. Government Printing Office, 1972), p. 73.

Unemployment insurance claimants must be available for full-time employment and must actively seek work. However, in some states veterans enrolled in school or training under the GI Bill may receive both their unemployment compensation payment and their GI Bill stipend. In other states, unemployment payments to GI Bill recipients are reduced. Still other state laws prohibit the collection of both.

Just as eligibility is determined by state law, so is the amount of the payment that the veteran receives. This level of payments is based upon the previous earnings of the unemployed worker. Because military cash payments are relatively low compared with civilian wages, federal law establishes presumed comparability to compensate for military in-kind compensation. This schedule yielded average weekly benefits of $56.34 per week in fiscal year 1972, almost equal to those paid to nonveterans.

In most states, the maximum duration of benefits is 26 weeks in any 52-week period, and federal law provides for extended benefits in states with high unemployment. But most veterans leave the unemployment rolls before they exhaust their benefits. In 1972, veterans qualifying for unemployment benefits remained on the rolls for 14.5 weeks, compared with the average claim of 14.4 weeks by nonveterans. The VA offers special help to those unemployed for long periods. After 12 weeks, the state unemployment insurance office notifies the VA of the veteran's status, and the agency again attempts to contact him to advise him of the sources of assistance available to help him find a job or place him in an education or training program.

The total amount of benefits paid increased more than tenfold between 1967 and 1972 (Chart 5). Not only has the average duration of veterans' claims and the average weekly benefits paid increased, the number of veterans establishing claims and collecting benefits has increased steadily. Two major factors account for this increase: (1) as a result of improved counseling, more Vietnam veterans have been made aware of the availability of unemployment compensation, and more importantly (2) unemployment benefits served as a buffer in a period when jobs were scarce during the recession.

Helping Veterans Find a Job

The veteran's readjustment began with counseling in the military or from the VA on what forms of employment or education were open to

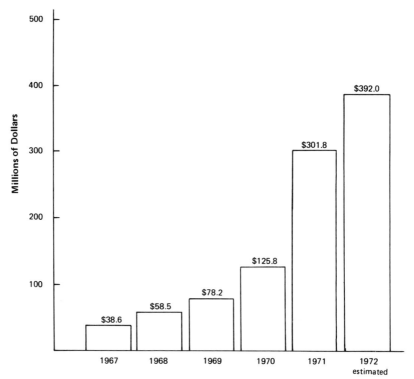

Source: Unemployment Insurance Service, U.S. Department of Labor (unpublished tables).

CHART 5. Approximately $1 Billion Has Been Paid in Unemployment Compensation to Ex-servicemen in the Past Six Years

him. If he had difficulty in finding employment, he could collect unemployment compensation to cushion his return to civilian life. The Harris survey[10] found that 55 percent of all Vietnam veterans collected unemployment benefits. To help the veteran find employment, the law provides him several direct routes to employment — reemployment rights in his preservice job, preference in civil service appointments, and special consideration under the U.S. Employment Service.

Reemployment Rights

To provide for men who left jobs to enter the military, reemployment rights for veterans have existed since 1940. Men and women who leave permanent jobs are eligible to return to the jobs and have their employee

---

[10] Louis Harris and Associates, Inc., *A Study of Problems, op. cit.*, p. 78.

benefits reinstated. In the case of disabled veterans, the Labor Department's Office of Reemployment Rights attempts to ensure that the incapacitated veteran is placed in a job that he is capable of performing. An employer is required to retain a veteran for at least one year unless the veteran is discharged for proper cause or is laid off.[11]

Generally veterans must apply for reemployment within 90 days of their discharge, although special extensions are available for the disabled. Altogether only 6,900 veterans contacted the Labor Department in 1971 for reemployment assistance. This represents less than 1 percent of all those who separated from the military during the year, and only about one of every 50 cases was referred to the Justice Department for litigation.[12] Most employers apparently cooperated with the law, and relatively few cases required public attention.

Preference in Civil Service Employment

Although veterans preference was traditional in federal government hiring practices before the end of World War II, the Veterans' Preference Act of 1944 clearly defined the civil service regulations for hiring veterans. Disabled veterans are eligible for an additional 10 points and other veterans for an extra 5 points on their civil service examination scores. If a veteran is disabled to the extent that he could not take a civil service appointment, his wife is eligible for his veterans preference rights. Widows of servicemen are also able to claim their husband's right to the preference if they should choose to enter federal employment. Other aspects of the law provide those claiming veterans preference with priority in reemployment and reinstatement in the federal civil service. And if a reduction in force should occur, they have preference over other employees in retaining their jobs.

Recent additions to veterans preference regulations for Vietnam veterans have made it easier for them to enter the federal civil srvice and to upgrade themselves. Since April 1970 federal agencies have been able to offer veterans noncompetitive appointments in jobs with an annual pay of $7,694 or less (grades 1 through 5, 1973 pay scales). These appointments are convertible to career positions, provided the

---

[11] Labor-Management Services Administration, U.S. Department of Labor, *Veterans' Reemployment Rights Handbook* (Washington, D.C.: U.S. Government Printing Office, 1970), pp. 1–14, 71–82.

[12] *Manpower Report of the President, 1971* (Washington, D.C.: U.S. Government Printing Office, 1971), pp. 62–63.

veteran completes a self-development program.[13] Appointments to jobs paying less than $6,128 (grade level 3 and below) can be made on the basis of the veteran's military experience, provided that the agency feels he can perform the duties of the job.

Of greater significance is the preference accorded veterans in state and local jobs, though practices vary widely. While federal employment remained relatively stable in recent years, state and local payrolls continued to expand even during the 1970 recession when aggregate private employment stagnated and even declined. In the first eight years of the Vietnam era, state and local employment rose by more than three million jobs. Vietnam veterans took advantage of the employment opportunities offered to them in public service, with blacks using their opportunities to a greater extent than whites. During mid-1971, 24 percent of employed black Vietnam veterans were in government jobs, compared with 12 percent of whites:[14]

	Percentage of whites	*Percentage of blacks*
Private wage and salary	85%	74%
Government	12%	24%
Self-employed and unpaid	4%	2%

In Search of a Job

Placement services of the more than 2,000 local offices of the U.S. Employment Service are available to all unemployed persons in search of jobs. Veterans have been singled out for special services since the Employment Service was established under the Wagner-Peyser Act in 1933. While other special groups have been spotlighted over the years for the attention of this agency, priority for veterans has been maintained.[15]

The majority of Vietnam veterans who have claimed unemployment benefits are also exposed to the public employment service, because most state laws require that persons collecting unemployment compensation

[13] Veterans Employment Service, U.S. Department of Labor, "Review and Analysis Report: The President's Veterans Program" (March 31, 1972) (mimeographed), p. 26.

[14] Elizabeth Waldman and Kathryn R. Gover, "Employment Situation of Vietnam Era Veterans," *Monthly Labor Review* (September 1971), p. 7. Percentage of whites does not total 100% because of rounding.

[15] Leonard P. Adams, *The Public Employment Service in Transition, 1933–1968* (Ithaca, N.Y.: New York State School of Industrial and Labor Relations, Cornell University, 1969), p. 43.

benefits sign up for work at the local employment service offices. But exposure to a local employment service may not help a veteran find employment, especially if employers fail to register their job vacancies or if the labor market information available is incomplete.

To augment the number of openings, Executive Order 11598 (June 18, 1971) required federal agencies and government contractors and subcontractors to list most job vacancies paying less than $18,000 annually with the local offices of the U.S. Employment Service. Veterans were to receive preference in referral to jobs.[16] It was hoped that 1.2 million such listings would be made available during the 1972 fiscal year. At the outset, programs were hampered by a slow start and surrounded by confusion as to what was actually required of the government contractors. Thus few jobs were registered in the "mandatory listings," and few Vietnam veterans benefited initially by the new policy.

During 1972, the U.S. Employment Service reported an increase in the number of nonagricultural jobs listed in its local offices for the first time in five years. And the number of placements of Vietnam veterans rose substantially over the previous year's performance. However, which portion of these improvements was due to the executive order and which to the revitalized veterans preference policies is uncertain.

---

[16] U.S. Department of Labor, "Listing of Job Vacancies with the Federal-State Employment System," *Federal Register* (September 14, 1971), vol. **XXXVI**, no. 178, pp. 18398–400.

Chapter 3.

Education and Training Benefits

Returning to an interrupted education or embarking on a new program for education or training is not easy for a 23-year-old veteran. Scholarship funds were often not as accessible to him as to the 18-year-old high school graduate. Lack of money or poor performance at school or a job may have been one of the major factors contributing to the initial drafting or enlistment of the veteran into the service. Even when funds were available to him, he had to compete with other veterans and nonveterans for woefully inadequate scholarship funds or loans. Parental financial aid, possibly available at 18, may not have been forthcoming for the older veteran, or may not be accepted. Although other problems contributed to choices other than the return to school, inadequate finances was a major factor which limited further education and training. Most did not need special services or other intensive or extensive efforts on their behalf — what they needed was money. Financial assistance for education and training of veterans returning to civilian society has been provided by the various GI Bills.

Education and training assistance constitute the largest single readjustment benefit for veterans both in amounts of money spent and in numbers of veterans making use of it. During the 26 years following World War II, some 13.5 million veterans have participated in education and training programs at a cost of more than $24.6 billion (Table 2).

The Vietnam Program

As of June 1972, some 3.1 million veterans had received education and training assistance under the 1966 GI Bill at a cost of $5.6 billion. Seven of 10 were Vietnam era veterans.[1] Another 267,000 servicemen received education or training assistance while in the military service. The number of veterans who turned to education and training during the early 1970s exceeded the participants during the preceding years. This occurred not only because their numbers increased, but also because job opportunities were scarce during the recession and its aftermath, and the government exerted special efforts to reach veterans who might be helped by the programs.

The veterans readjustment program is flexible in allowing the veteran his choice in selecting a program of education and training and the method of completing that program. Within broad guidelines the program offers income support and leaves to the veterans the selection of training, educational courses, and facilities. The law distinguishes be-

Table 2

The Three GI Bills Have Provided Education Benefits to 13.5 Million Veterans at a Cost of $24.6 Billion

Time Period	Eligible (million)	Trained (million)	Cost (billion)
At end of World War II	15.6	7.8	$14.5
At end of Korean Conflict	5.7	2.4	4.5
Post-Korean Conflict[a]	9.1	3.3	5.6
Total	30.4	13.5	$24.6

[a] As of June 1972.

Source: Department of Veterans Benefits, Veterans Administration, *Veterans Benefits under Current Educational Programs* (June 1972), Information Bulletin no. 24-72-6, p. 30; "Veterans Affairs," *Congress and the Nation, 1965–1968* (Washington, D.C.: Congressional Quarterly, Inc., 1969), p. 456.

---

[1] Department of Veterans Benefits, Veterans Administration, *Veterans Benefits under Current Educational Programs* (June 1972), Information Bulletin no. 24-72-6, p. 7.

tween institutional education or training and on-the-job training (OJT) programs.

Most of the post-Korean veterans have applied their GI Bill benefits to college-level courses, while only a little more than 1 percent of the trainees have returned to high school. The others are distributed among vocational, OJT, and correspondence courses. Farm training has attracted less than 10,000 of the 3.1 million trainees (Table 3).

TABLE 3

More Than Three Million Veterans Enrolled in Education and Training Programs between 1966 and June 1972[a]

Type of Training	Number Enrolled (thousands)	Percentage of Enrollees
Higher education:		
Graduate	290	9.5%
Undergraduate	1,366	44.6
Nondegree	23	0.8
Correspondence course	7	0.2
Total in higher education	1,687	55.0
Below college level:		
Vocational/technical	442	14.4
High school	39	1.3
Flight training	75	2.4
Farm	9	0.3
Correspondence course	551	18.0
Total in below college level	1,115	36.4
On-the-job training:		
Apprenticeship	150	4.9
Other	114	3.7
Total on-the-job training	264	8.6
Total enrollment in all three categories[b]	3,066	100.0%

[a] Details may not add to totals because of rounding.

[b] Excludes 60,000 servicemen enrolled in higher education and 207,000 in below college programs.

Source: Department of Veterans Benefits, Veterans Administration, *Veterans Benefits under Current Educational Programs* (June 1972), Information Bulletin no. 24-72-6, Appendix Table 3, p. 20.

PROGRAM ADMINISTRATION AND MONITORING

The Education and Rehabilitation Service of the Department of Veterans Benefits is responsible for the administration of education and training benefits. The actual processing of applications for educational benefits is the responsibility of the adjudication divisions of the regional offices. Their staff members assist the veteran in choosing a program and in filing the proper application.

Consistent with its philosophy, the VA relies on existing facilities, institutions, or businesses for the education and training of veterans. Although a veteran is free to choose his own program of education or training, experience demonstrated that certain safeguards were necessary to assure that the veteran received responsible training and that the taxpayers' dollars were spent beneficially. The law requires that financial assistance can be awarded for enrollment only in approved courses or training programs. The right to approve courses is reserved for an appropriate agency in the state where the institution offering the program is located. The VA reimburses these state approving agencies for their services. In 1972 the VA had contracts with 69 such agencies, at an annual cost of $8 million.

The governor of each state designates one or more approving agencies. In states with two agencies, the most common arrangement is to assign to the department of education the responsibility for approval of institutional training and to the Labor Department the apprenticeship and other OJT programs. Professional accreditation associations help the approving agencies in decisions concerning the institutional courses.

After the state approving agency makes the decision on the adequacy of the quality of the courses, institutions, and training programs, final determination of whether the course of study offers a "program of education" as defined in the law rests with the VA. Although the definition is very liberal, it does exclude various recreational or avocational courses. To avoid fly-by-night institutions, the guidelines require that a proprietary school at below college level must have offered a course for two years before a veteran is eligible to enroll and receive benefits. Also, no more than 85 percent of the students in a nonaccredited course may be veterans.

The VA has retained the responsibility for direct approval in several instances. Schools or courses in foreign countries, training in federal agencies, and programs offered by interstate carriers such as airlines or railroads are approved by the VA rather than the state approving agencies.

It is difficult to assess the impact of these approving and monitoring measures on the quality of the programs which the veteran enters. Professional accreditation and government training standards are followed in assessing quality or adequacy, and even accreditation or minimum standards do not automatically lead to approval. One can be certain that many of the institutional programs or training courses may be of questionable quality and marginal benefit to the veteran, thereby wasting the veteran's time and the public's dollars. It is also certain, however, that these safeguard measures, although less than stringent, assure greater protection and higher quality programs than those available to the general public, where legal safeguards are minimal at most.

Generally, the institutions or establishments offering the program have very little contact or relationship with the VA beyond the initial approval process. Educational institutions process veterans much as they do nonveterans, and they receive a nominal reimbursement at a rate of $3.00 per veteran enrolled for the extra paperwork. Training establishments with OJT programs must also verify monthly hours worked and wages earned, but the paperwork and mailing is handled by the veteran, and there is no reimbursement.

ELIGIBILITY AND INSTITUTIONS

One paramount facet of the GI Bills has been their near universality in coverage of veterans. Although the present eligibility requirements are somewhat more restrictive than in the past, the concept of universal eligibility for veterans with substantial service remains intact.

As defined by the Veterans Educational Assistance Act, to be eligible a veteran qualifies for benefits if he

(1) Served on active duty in the Armed Forces for a period of more than 180 days, any part of which occurred after January 31, 1955

(2) Was discharged for a service-connected disability

(3) Was discharged under conditions other than dishonorable

The 181-day service requirement was designed to exclude the reservists serving less than six months of active duty in the Armed Forces.

A veteran is eligible for benefits for eight years after the date of his discharge. Exceptions are made to this general regulation for veterans who were discharged before the passage of the law in 1966, and for veterans whose discharge status has undergone a change since separation.

For each month of service a veteran is eligible to receive 1.5 months of full-time education or training assistance. The minimum period of service, six months, entitles a veteran to benefits for nine months. Once the period of service reaches 18 months, the veteran automatically becomes entitled to the maximum 36 months' assistance.

Of the nearly 1.2 million Vietnam era veterans receiving training allowances in April 1972, more than six of 10 enrolled in institutions of higher learning (Table 4). The number of Vietnam era veterans choosing to enroll in institutions of higher learning has been increasing. About one in seven of those attending institutions of higher learning were doing post-graduate work, and about 40 percent attended junior or community colleges. The popularity of these colleges is largely due to the relative inexpensiveness of these schools, the proximity to veterans' residences, and the wide variety of courses, both in academic pursuits and in training for technical or trade fields.

Veterans enrolled in some 4,800 institutions of higher learning in 1971. One-third of these were public institutions, and two-thirds were private. When the number of veterans enrolled is taken into consideration, however, the ratio is reversed, with almost 80 percent enrolled in public institutions, compared with 48 percent of the World War II veterans who enrolled in public institutions. The greater availability of public institutions and the soaring costs of education in private institutions largely explain this shift.

The VA permits veterans maximum discretion in their choices of educational or training programs. The agency therefore maintains only casual data about the academic pursuits of enrollees. In the absence of operational needs, the VA has no records about the courses pursued by a majority of enrollees.

College-level training has accounted for nearly three of every four institutional enrollments. More than 25 percent of all veterans receiving benefits for readjustment training were enrolled in over 6,000 institutions below the college level.

TABLE 4

Almost 1.2 Million Veterans Were Enrolled in Education and Training
Programs under the GI Bill in April 1972[a]

Type of Training	Number Enrolled (thousands)	Percentage of Enrollees
Higher education:		
Graduate	104	8.9%
Undergraduate	637	54.7
Nondegree	5	0.5
Correspondence course	3	0.3
Total in higher education	748	64.4
Below college level:		
Vocational/technical	86	7.4
High school	12	1.0
Flight training	20	1.7
Farm	7	0.6
Correspondence course	194	16.7
Total in less than college level	319	27.4
On-the-job training:		
Apprenticeship	61	5.2
Other	35	3.0
Total in on-the-job training	96	8.2
Total enrollment in all three categories[b]	1,164	100.0%

[a] Details may not add to totals because of rounding.

[b] Does not include 82,000 servicemen.

Source: Department of Veterans Benefits, Veterans Administration, *Veterans Benefits under Current Educational Programs* (June 24, 1972), Information Bulletin no. 24-72-4, Appendix Table 1.

As in the college-level program, the number of below college-level private institutions enrolling veterans predominate by almost a three-to-one margin. Unlike the college program, however, the private institutions also account for more than 85 percent of veterans enrolled, compared with 20 percent in the college program. The preference for private institutions reflects primarily the dearth of public educational or training facilities below the college level and the wide range of fees and tuition costs that are frequently within the reach of veterans.

TRAINING COURSES

Vocational and technical training of veterans in below college-level training concentrated heavily in technical, business and commerce, and trade and industrial courses (Chart 6). These three areas accounted for 75 to 80 percent of all persons enrolled. Electronics technicians accounted for about four-fifths of the veterans in the technical courses. Accounting, computer technology, and real estate or insurance were the major business interests (over 50 percent) and air conditioning, electronic trades, and mechanical courses (largely automotive) accounted for more than three-fifths of those in trade and industrial pursuits.

These distributions indicate that veterans, to a large extent, entered courses which offer good futures. Computer technology, accounting, electronics, and automotive mechanics are generally fields where there has been and should continue to be a growing demand for labor in a tight labor market.

Of the servicemen leaving the military each year, approximately 20 percent have not completed their high school education. The VA estimates that as of June 1972, 284,000 veterans and 29,000 servicemen without high school credentials entered training under the 1966 GI Bill. Most entered vocational and OJT courses not requiring high school completion. This is to be expected, since the VA policy of allowing the veteran a free choice in selecting his program of studies does not necessarily emphasize the importance of high school education.

Under the World War II GI Bill, all stipends were charged against the veterans' educational entitlement. To motivate veterans who had not completed high school, the 1970 amendments to the 1966 Bill qualified them to enroll in secondary education courses without reducing their entitlement, provided they needed these courses to qualify for further training. This provision enables the veteran to complete high school and continue through four years of college work, all under the GI Bill.

Veterans using the so-called "free entitlement" for high school and college preparatory classes may receive payments for tutorial assistance for nine months at not more than $50 per month in addition to the regular institutional stipends. As of June 1972, some 89,000 veterans and 19,000 servicemen had taken advantage of the free entitlement. Most of the trainees enrolled in high school courses, although some were in college taking noncredit courses to prepare them for the standard cur-

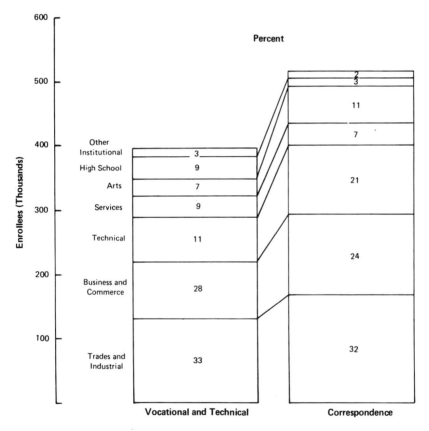

Source: Veterans Administration, *Schools below the College Level (Cumulative from June 1, 1966, through June 30, 1971)* (mimeographed) and *Correspondence Courses in Schools below College Level (Cumulative through 1971)* (mimeographed).

CHART 6. Distribution of Veterans and Servicemen in Below College-Level Courses, 1966–71

riculum. "Free entitlement" widens the options of educationally disadvantaged veterans and may have encouraged some of the 89,000
veterans to complete their high school education before embarking on a
vocational education career or continuing their higher education.

CORRESPONDENCE COURSES

Data on below college-level training must be used with considerable
caution since more than 50 percent of the veterans and serivcemen enrolled in this level of training have enrolled in correspondence courses of
questionable merit (Chart 6). In fact, approximately one-sixth of all
trainees have enrolled in such courses at a cost of $237 million in benefits
under the current GI Bill. Enrollment in these courses grew by more
than one-third during fiscal year 1971, compared with less than one-
fifth growth in college enrollments.

Despite their popularity, correspondence courses and the problems
connected with them have been given considerable attention. Correspondence courses must be approved by the National Home Study
Council, designated by the U.S. Department of Health, Education and
Welfare as the accrediting agency for such courses, or by the state
approving agency where the school is located. A General Accounting
Office (GAO) study, however, has pointed out that accreditation does
not prevent problems. The study suggests that correspondence courses
may not be good investments for either the veteran's time or the public's
money.[2]

Of the 212,000 veterans who were no longer receiving educational
assistance payments for correspondence courses at the end of fiscal year
1970, some 160,000 had not completed their courses. Some dropouts
reported to the GAO that the courses were too time consuming or too
difficult to be practicable for them. Others said that they lost interest or
that the course did not fulfill their expectations. Of those who failed to
complete correspondence courses, 57 percent stated that they would
have chosen a different form of education if they had been aware before
they started of the difficulties they would face in order to complete the
course of study.

Enrolling in correspondence courses can also become expensive for
veterans, especially if they do not complete the course. Because the VA

---

[2] U.S. General Accounting Office, *Most Veterans Not Completing Correspondence Courses* (March 22, 1972), no. B-114859, pp. 8–9.

reimburses the enrollees in quarterly payments only for completed lessons, the veteran normally must invest his own money in advance. Responding to criticism by the GAO study, the 1972 law established a refund policy and a 10-day cooling off period for correspondence enrollees. Previously veterans dropping out of a school accredited by the National Home Study Council paid a fixed percentage of the charge for the course or a pro rata charge for the lessons completed, whichever was greater. If the course was not nationally accredited, the charge could not exceed the approximate pro rata charge of completed lessons.

According to the GAO study, veterans and servicemen who dropped out of correspondence courses incurred an average cost of $180. Of the dropouts, 31 percent did not know that the VA reimbursement would not cover their costs if they did not complete the course, and most were not aware that they would have to request a refund if they were eligible for one. Veterans now have a 10-day period during which they can drop out of the course subject only to a charge of 10 percent of the cost of the course, or a $50 registration fee, whichever is less. If a veteran completes less than 25 or 50 percent of the course, he must pay the registration fee plus 25 or 50 percent of the cost of the course, respectively. Veterans who complete more than one-half of the course before terminating receive no refund.

Refunds are not the only source of frustration to correspondence enrollees. Information gathered by the VA shows that many veterans feel that the claims of adequate vocational training and employment opportunities by the course sponsors are exaggerated. Other veterans complained of the questionable business practices or even illegal activities of some sponsors. These included sponsors using the VA seal on promotion literature, claiming that courses had "VA accreditation," and inducing the veteran to sign a loan application while purporting to be making his application for enrollment.[3]

Because the veteran's entitlement is reduced by one month for each $220 paid to him by the VA, his aggregate entitlement is reduced when he pursues a correspondence course. In order to discourage frivolous use of entitlement for correspondence courses, the 1972 law required that veterans pay 10 percent of the cost. The provision is an attempt to put

---

[3] *Congressional Record* (daily edition, August 3, 1972), p. S12648.

the veteran in the same position as enrollees in most other institutional courses who must fund part of their own educational expenses.

SPECIALIZED TRAINING

The law provides some specialized training. Farm training is available to veterans who own or manage a farm or have prospects of doing so. To be eligible for education benefits, veterans in a farm program must take institutional courses related to farm operations in conjunction with actual farm experience. Until October 1972, a post-Korean veteran with no dependents was required to take a minimum of 12 hours of institutional training each week for 44 weeks (528 hours during the year) to be eligible to receive the full-time training stipend.

Few young veterans have turned recently to farm training. The decline in agricultural employment and the erosion of the community-based agricultural extension courses were largely responsible for this drastic decrease. Under World War II and Korean GI Bills, the participation rates for veterans in farm training were 3.6 and 1.7 percent, respectively. In April 1972, only 0.3 percent of veterans receiving training stipends were participating in farm training. And this was almost triple the number enrolled the previous April. Several farm lobbies have argued that the requirement for institutional coursework may have contributed to the decline. Although modern management and technical skills are generally recognized as necessary for the contemporary farmer, there was support in Congress and among the farm organizations for reducing the institutional training. Under the provisions of the October 1972 Readjustment Act, a full-time farm program consists of 10 hours per week or 440 hours per year with no less than 80 clock hours in any three-month period.[4] The presumed justification for the relaxed training standards is to encourage more veterans to train in farm management and to contribute to the continuation of viable family farms. The argument is not necessarily persuasive. It is difficult to assess which part of the recent decrease in the interest in farm training may be due to the institutional requirements added to the 1966 law and which part may be due to a decline in agricultural employment. And it is not at all clear that the relaxed training standards will improve the farm population.

---

[4] VIETNAM ERA VETERANS' READJUSTMENT ASSISTANCE ACT OF 1972 (October 24, 1972), Public Law 92-540, § 303.

Flight training, another type of specialized training authorized by the veterans readjustment legislation, was more popular. By June 1972, some 75,000 veterans had taken flight training, and almost one-half of these received benefits during fiscal year 1972. To be entitled to flight training, a veteran must hold a private pilot's license and be able to show how further flight training will help his present career or contribute to some employment objective. He can only attend a school which is approved by both the Federal Aviation Agency and the state approving agency.

Most of the veterans who enter flight training complete the course, according to the VA. Moreover, nine of 10 completers continue to take advanced courses in instrument rating and multi-engines.[5] However, the VA has not published any data about the extent that flight training serves as preparation for employment or for avocational pursuits.

On-the-Job Training

The GI Bill also makes provision for training veterans in a non-institutional setting. In providing for veterans who seek OJT, Congress has faced the perennial problem in this type of situation of assuring that the assistance would go to aid the intended clients of the program rather than to subsidize employers.

As with other education benefits, OJT must be approved by the state approving agency and must be designed to provide for upward occupational mobility. If a veteran desires to enter OJT under an employer not approved by the state approving agency, he is free to encourage the employer to apply for approval. As a condition of approval, the wages paid by the employer to the veteran must be no less than those paid to nonveterans training for the same position and must at least equal 50 percent of the journeyman's rate. The wage schedule must also provide progression to 85 percent of the journeyman wage prior to the completion of the training period.

In addition to the wage requirements, the training must be structured to last between six and 24 months. The length should be equivalent to that of comparable establishments for comparable jobs. And

---

[5] House Subcommittee on Education and Training, Committee of Veterans' Affairs, 92d Cong., 1st Sess., "Hearings on Education and Training Programs Administered by the Veterans Administration" (November 30, 1971) (Washington, D.C.: U.S. Government Printing Office, 1972), pp. 1563–64.

finally, there must be a reasonable assurance that the target job will be available to the veteran when he completes the training.

The state approving agency is responsible for investigating OJT programs to assure that the content of the training and facilities are adequate to prepare the veteran for his job objective. The veteran is obligated to keep a record of his progress each month, which must be signed by the employer and submitted to the VA.

Apprenticeship programs for veterans must meet the guidelines set by the Secretary of Labor for such training.[6] To be "recognized," an apprenticeship program must be registered with the state approving agency or with the Bureau of Apprenticeship and Training of the Labor Department.

Less than 10 percent of the veterans receiving education and training benefits have opted for OJT or apprenticeship (see Table 4). During 1972 the VA began a special outreach program to attract OJT trainees. Visits to more than 100,000 employers opened over 84,000 OJT slots during the year. Although the future impact of the new effort is uncertain, it resulted in a growth in OJT enrollments over the traditionally more popular apprenticeship programs during 1972.

EDUCATION AND TRAINING BENEFITS

The payments made to veterans enrolled in education and training programs are in the nature of a supplemental stipend rather than a wage to support the veteran and his dependents. Having determined that the readjustment stipend is not to be considered a subsistance wage, Congress lacked any criteria for establishing a "proper" level of benefits. The amount paid to a single veteran attending full-time school between 1970 and 1972, the period when most of the Vietnam veterans entered civilian life, was $175 per month. Effective in October 1972, the basic benefit for enrollees was raised to $220 per month. Recognizing that a veteran with dependents had greater financial responsibilities and added difficulties in pursuing a course of education and training than a single veteran, Congress raised the stipend for a veteran with a single dependent to $261 a month and to $298 for a veteran with two dependents. The stipend was boosted by another $18 for each additional dependent.

---

[6] Manpower Administration, U.S. Department of Labor, *The National Apprenticeship Program* (Washington, D.C.: U.S. Government Printing Office, 1968), p. 6.

An enrollee in an educational training program was deemed to be entitled to a full-time stipend if the veteran attended a training program for 30 or more hours, or if he was enrolled in a college for at least 14 semester hours or its equivalent. Part-time enrollees received proportionate payment. For example, a single student enrolled for 10 to 13 semester hours was entitled to three-fourths of the full-time stipend, or $165 a month. Similarly, a single veteran enrolled in seven to nine hours received $110 a month. The monthly educational assistance allowances paid to veterans enrolled in institutional programs as of October 1972 are shown in Table 5.

Given the arbitrary determination of allowances, comparison with benefits paid to World War II and Korean GIs was inevitable. Precise comparisons are difficult because of changed provisions. It would seem, however, that World War II veterans had a better deal than their Vietnam successors. The unmarried World War II veteran enrolled in institutional training received a monthly allowance of $75 plus up to $500 per year for tuition, paid directly to the institution in which the veteran was enrolled. The amount was adequate to cover the tuition charged at that time by most schools, and the veteran was left with his allowance.

As the cost of education rose, the VA arrangements became a considerable burden to educational institutions, particularly publicly supported facilities. Even in private institutions, tuition does not normally cover actual costs, and the students are subsidized. In the public institu-

TABLE 5

Monthly Institutional Benefits

Category	Dependents			For Each Additional Dependent
	None	One	Two	
Full-time enrollee	$220	$261	$298	$18
Three-quarter-time enrollee	$165	$196	$224	$14
Half-time enrollee[a]	$110	$131	$149	$ 9

[a] The allowance for veterans enrolled on less than a half-time basis or for servicemen on active duty cannot exceed the established tuition and fee charges that nonveterans pay in the same course, or the above rate established at $220 for a full-time enrollee, whichever is less.

Source: Vietnam Era Veterans' Readjustment Assistance Act of 1972 (October 24, 1972), Public Law 92-450.

tions, tuition is minimal if not token, and the students are of course subsidized from public revenue. The VA reimbursement under World
War II arrangements therefore placed the burden on education and
training institutions — since the government allowances encouraged
veterans to undertake education and training programs — but the VA
payment did not cover the actual cost of training. Attempts to assess
the costs for enrolling and training veterans proved unsuccessful, and
the direct payment for expenses to the school was discontinued. Instead
the government was to give the veteran a uniform allowance and to leave
it to the trainee to pay whatever tuition the institution charged to other
students.

The cash stipend paid to the Vietnam veteran, even after it was
adjusted for changes in cost of living, still exceeded in 1972 the amounts
paid to the World War II and Korean veterans. Adjusted for 1972
prices, the $75 monthly payment of the World War II veteran in 1948
equaled $131. The $110 paid to the Korean veteran in 1954, adjusted
for rises in cost of living, amounted to $172 and was very close to the
amount received by the Vietnam veteran during most of 1972. But an
analysis of comparative payments to the veterans of the three wars
should also take into consideration the overall increase in productivity
and standard of living and not just the increase in the cost of living.
From these calculations, it appears that society treated the World War II
veteran more favorably than his successors during the two "unofficial"
wars. Between 1948 and June 1972, per capita disposable income in
the United States rose by 191 percent. With this as the criterion, the
$75 a month allowance to the single World War II veterans in 1948
should have been raised to $218 for Vietnam veterans.

Although the basic benefit for Vietnam veterans was raised to $220
in October 1972, the government did not pay any tuition for the Korean
or Vietnam veteran. About three of every four Vietnam veterans enrolled in public colleges, but in 1972 they still had to pay an average
annual tuition in these public institutions of $383.[7] This tuition, sub-
tracted from the $1,575 annual stipend (based on a nine-month school
year), left the veteran with about $130 a month while he was attending
school. A veteran who chose to attend a private school had to pay an

---

[7] U.S. Bureau of the Census, *Statistical Abstract of the United States, 1971*
(Washington, D.C.: U.S. Government Printing Office, 1971), p. 126.

average tuition fee of $255 in excess of the total allowance he received from the government (the average tuition in private schools in 1972 was $1,830). Receiving increased benefits and paying greater tuition, veterans in public schools will be somewhat better off during 1973. Paying an average tuition of $392 from $1,980 in allowances will leave him $188 per month. The veteran in a private school will receive benefits only slightly greater than his $1,919 tuition bill.

The above calculations do not consider, however, the duration of benefits which tended to favor Vietnam veterans. World War II veterans received one month of educational allowances for each month served on active duty, up to 48 months. Because most served lengthy tours of duty, they qualified for maximum benefits. Vietnam and Korean veterans were entitled to 1.5 months of educational allowances for each month of service, and those serving 18 months have been eligible for the maximum entitlement of 36 months, giving them sufficient time to complete the normal college course.

The Vietnam veteran enrolled in a college or in institutional training was in a position to pyramid benefits, and some did. Funds under the Education Professions Development Act, the Educational Talent Search, the Career Opportunities program, and the Teacher Corps are available to those pursuing post-secondary education in the fields of elementary, high school, and college teaching, administration, and counseling. Since March 1970, veterans have been eligible to receive GI Bill education benefits concurrent with federal fellowship aid. During fiscal year 1972, the U.S. Office of Education estimated that a little more than $17 million would be spent to assist approximately 4,500 veterans in these programs.[8] In addition, other veterans received Equal Opportunity Grants, College Work Study, National Defense Education Act Student Loans, or Guaranteed Student Loans to support their college training.

The veteran who chooses institutional, noncollege training may be no better off than the one who attends college. Duration of training and costs of vocational and technical training vary widely. In order to qualify for full-time benefits of $220 a month, the veteran would have

---

[8] Taken from a statement made by Sidney P. Marland, Jr., Commissioner of the U.S. Office of Education, to the Senate Committee on Veterans' Affairs, 92d Cong., April 28, 1972 (mimeographed).

to attend upward of 100 hours of training. The tuition fee alone would therefore be about equal to the total allowances received by the veteran. As with college students, vocational and technical trainees must bear the costs of books and supplies as well as living expenses.

A modest work study provision added in the 1972 law offers assistance to veterans who cannot meet the full costs of their education. Funding is limited to approximately 16,000 veterans at a cost of $4 million each year. A needy veteran can receive up to $250 in advance for agreeing to work 100 hours for the VA. Not only is the program intended to help veterans who need part-time work during the school year, it is also to assist the VA regional offices in their outreach efforts to aid other veterans, the processing of paperwork for the education program, or for work in VA medical facilities.[9]

Another 1972 provision to ease the financial burden on the veteran at the beginning of the school term was the advance payment of educational assistance allowances to cover costs of books, supplies, and registration fees. A veteran who is at least a half-time student can receive the amount due him during the month he starts school, plus the following month's stipend. During subsequent months, the veteran receives prepaid allowances so long as he submits proof of enrollment and satisfactory progress. Part-time students taking less than half-time courses can receive a lump sum allowance for the term after the VA receives certification of enrollment.

The World War II experience provided only a negative guideline for the payment of benefits for on-site training. The initial GI Bill of 1944 imposed a limit on the earnings of veterans in OJT. While in training, an unmarried veteran was allowed a maximum monthly income of $210, including both OJT payments and wages. The wage paid to the veteran for a maximum of two years did not affect his income since it was reduced by an amount equal to every increase in his wages. When his monthly wages reached $210, he was disqualified from receiving further allowances. The arrangement robbed the veteran of incentives to secure higher wages, and frequently ended up as a subsidy to the employer rather than as a supplement to the veteran.

To remedy this situation, the 1955 law provided Korean veterans

---

[9] Vietnam Era Veterans' Readjustment Assistance Act of 1972 (October 24, 1972), Public Law 92-540, §§ 201 and 203.

with a $70 per month allowance which was reduced at regular four-month intervals, anticipating periodic increases in the trainee's wages. The ceiling on monthly income was removed to allow veterans to press for wage increases due them. The present law requires that employers pay veterans the same wage rate as they pay nonveterans for the same job and that they at least pay the federal minimum wage of $1.60 per hour. For post-Korean veterans, OJT payments are reduced at six-month intervals (Table 6).

The OJT allowance therefore serves as an incentive for the veteran to undertake training by supplementing his income during the period of training, since his income from apprenticeship may frequently be below that which he might get from the open market for other jobs. The allowance may serve to compensate the veteran for foregone earnings deferred as a result of his undertaking training. Though data are not available, the allowance may also provide an incentive to the employer to hire veterans . . . since the lure of higher wages elsewhere frequently encourages trainees or apprentices to drop out before completing their formal course of training. The wage supplement provided by the government to the veteran may encourage more stable employment prospects.

While the 1972 law effected a 25.7 percent increase in the basic allowance paid to veterans studying at institutions and in farm programs, the increase in the basic OJT benefit was 48.1 percent. This increase represents an attempt to correct a traditional bias which favors

TABLE 6

Monthly On-the-Job and Apprenticeship Benefits

	Dependents			For Each Additional Dependent
Category	None	One	Two	
First six months	$160	$179	$196	$8
Second six months	120	139	156	8
Third six months	80	99	116	8
Fourth six months and succeeding periods	$ 40	$ 52	$ 76	$8

Source: VIETNAM ERA VETERANS' READJUSTMENT ASSISTANCE ACT OF 1972 (October 24, 1972), Public Law 92-540.

institutional programs of study. Under the provisions effective between
1970 and 1972, a single OJT trainee working 40 hours per week all year
could earn approximately $4,500 per year in wages and allowances, even
if his wages were not increased after the first six months. The new provision will raise the annual income of the same trainee above $5,000
($3,328 in wages and $1,680 in allowances). A married veteran with
two dependents would receive almost $5,500 a year.

Little is known about the quality of training offered to veterans
under OJT. In the absence of hard data, it may be surmised that some
employers misused the allowance system to hire veterans at lower wages.
Also the OJT programs are not required to include a minimum number
of employees or to have been in business for two years before receiving
approval. Such loose requirements do little to assure meaningful training. However, the employer's certification that there is "reasonable certainty" that the veteran will have a job after being trained and that his
wages during the last six months of training will be 85 percent of the job
for which he is being trained are generally thought to assure that the
training will pay off in employment for the veteran.

COSTS OF TRAINING

Except for the amounts paid in veterans' benefits each year, little
information is available on the expenditures involved in administering
educational readjustment for veterans. The average stipend paid to each
veteran enrolled for training during 1972 was $972, a small increase over
the two preceding years (Table 7). Most of the increase each year is due
to the increasing proportion of full-time enrollees — from 48 percent in
April 1970 to 59 percent in April 1972. Another factor was the slight
increase (from 39 percent in April 1970 to 43 percent in April 1972)
in the percentage of enrollees with dependents. Longer periods of training and the rising costs of flight training and correspondence courses
were other additions to the increased costs. Further increases are anticipated with the boosts in the level of benefits.

Higher education absorbed 72 percent of the total outlays in 1972,
though college students accounted for only 56 percent of enrollment.
Veterans attending college were paid an average of $1,233 per student,
compared with $598 received by the trade and technical students. The
differences in payments were due to the fact that the vast majority of

TABLE 7

Outlays for Veterans' Education and Training Programs
Exceeded $1.8 Billion in 1972

Type of Training	Number of Trainees	Unit Cost	Total Cost (thousands)
Higher education:			
Graduate	170,359	$1,101	$ 187,650
Undergraduate	894,154	1,258	1,124,869
Junior college	(389,900)	(1,169)	(455,742)
Other education:			
High school	39,973	420	16,789
Trade or technical school	546,458	558	305,010
On-the-job training	161,683	734	118,623
Flight training	42,647	1,029	43,893
Cooperative farm	8,884	1,748	15,529
Educationally disadvantaged	(67,201)	(390)	(26,208)
Servicemen	(139,908)	(345)	(48,308)
Correspondence	(282,292)	(396)	(111,754)
Total	1,864,158	$ 972	$1,812,434

a Figures in parentheses are non-add items shown in other detail.

Source: Prepared by the Management and Budget Service, Veterans Administration (October 31, 1972) (unpublished document).

trade school enrollees qualified for only part-time or correspondence course payments, while most college students received full-time stipends. In contrast, the average amount spent on educationally disadvantaged veterans was only $390. These educationally disadvantaged veterans were those who used the "free entitlement" to take refresher courses. The $390 payment represented only the initial investment in their training since they were expected to move into college and vocational courses during succeeding years.

TRAINEE CHARACTERISTICS

More than half the Vietnam trainees were 25 years or older — an age when most other adults are already set on a career. The "advanced" age of the veteran-trainee reflects the two years or more "lost" in the service, and the special inducements the government offers to the veteran may attract young adults to return to school.

The typical trainee graduated from high school before entering the Armed Forces. Veterans who had dropped out of school before graduation from high school have tended to take less advantage of the educational and training benefits than those with a high school education. While one of every five veterans had failed to graduate from high school, only 8 percent of those enrolled in educational training programs had less than a high school education (Chart 7). A study[10] of all enlisted reservists — two of every three persons separated — for the three-year period ending in 1971 disclosed that 34.5 percent entered some form of training or educational program. The participation rate was highest for veterans who had some college education before entering the service, but who had not graduated. Those with less than a high school education before entering the service had the lowest participation rate.

Participation rates of blacks were lower than those of whites. While more than one of every three whites received educational training benefits, only one-fourth of the blacks participated in these programs. Except for those with less than a high school education, the proportion of blacks who received education and training benefits was lower in every other educational category than for that of whites (Chart 8). It would seem that the traditional "color blind" policy of VA has not resulted in blacks reaping their proportion of the benefits of the GI Bill.

The lower participation rates of the deficiently educated and black in the GI Bill may also reflect a bias inherent in the legislation. The law favors those attending college as compared with those participating in technical or vocational training. The veteran who is attending a college course receives benefits for full-time training for the minimal number of hours which is considered a full-time course load at that institution. The veteran who is enrolled in a technical or vocational program, however, must meet weekly course hour requirements and is subject to a more stringent reporting procedure attesting to his attendance. The college student is given considerable leeway to augment his income since his schedule of 14 credit hours is considered full-time work, thus permitting

---

[10] Human Resources Research Organization, "DOD Post-Service Analysis of Men Separating 1 July 1968–31 December 1970" (unpublished data).

Education Level

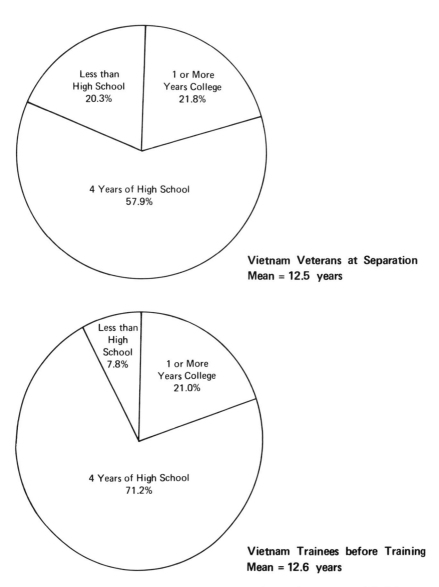

Less than
High School
20.3%

1 or More
Years College
21.8%

4 Years of High School
57.9%

**Vietnam Veterans at Separation
Mean = 12.5 years**

Less than
High
School
7.8%

1 or More
Years College
21.0%

4 Years of High School
71.2%

**Vietnam Trainees before Training
Mean = 12.6 years**

Source: All Vietnam veterans: Reports and Statistics Service, Veterans Administration, *Data on Vietnam Era Veterans* (June 1972), p. 7; Vietnam trainees: Department of Veterans Benefits, Veterans Administration, *Veterans Benefits under Current Educational Programs* (June 1972), Information Bulletin no. 24-72-6, p. 32.

CHART 7. The Most Deficiently Educated Veterans Tended Not to
Enroll in GI Bill Programs, Cumulative to June 1972

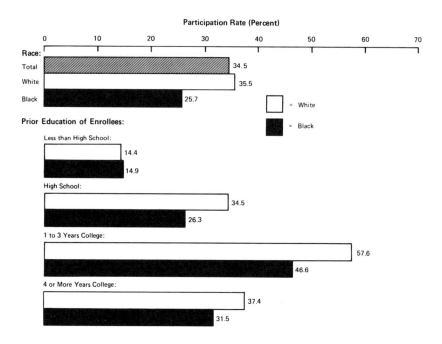

Source: Human Resources Research Organization, "DOD Post-Service Analysis of Men Separating 1 July 1968–31 December 1970" (unpublished data).

CHART 8. Blacks Were Represented Less Than Whites in GI Bill Programs, Those Who Separated between July 1, 1968, and December 31, 1970

the student to seek part-time employment. The veteran enrolled in a vocational or technical course must, however, attend institutional training for at least 25 and sometimes 30 hours a week in order to qualify for full-time allowances.[11] The inequity becomes apparent in the case of two veterans enrolled in the same classes but with different degree objectives. Both veterans may be enrolled in mathematics and electronics courses, but the veteran enrolled for a degree has to be enrolled in 14 credit hours in order to get his full benefits, while the veteran who rakes these courses in order to qualify for, say, electronics equipment repair does not qualify for full-time benefits unless he has at least a 25-hour schedule of institutional training.

---

[11] Kenneth B. Hoyt, "Career Education and Career Choice: Implications for the Veterans Administration" (February 8, 1972), address to the National Task Force on Education and the Vietnam Era Veteran, Veterans Administration, pp. 12–13.

VA participation data clearly indicate rising emphasis of college education under the GI Bill. Less than one of every three World War II veterans who participated in training were enrolled in college, compared with nearly six of 10 post-Korean veterans (Chart 9). The lower enrollment rate of the high school dropout may reflect the lack of interest in added formal education or skills training, but it may also reflect the biases in the law which tend to offer him less benefits than the degree-bound student. Also, the counseling offered to most veterans is inadequate for them to formulate a career education plan, and veterans tend

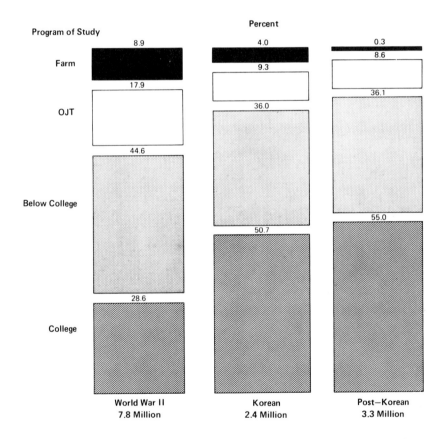

Source: Department of Veterans Benefits, Veterans Administration, *Veterans Benefits under Current Educational Programs* (June 1972), Information Bulletin no. 24-72-6, p. 30.

CHART 9. The Proportion of Veterans Enrolling in College under the GI Bill Doubled Since World War II

to gravitate to college courses frequently without a clear vocational objective.

It may be questioned whether the bias in favor of the degree-bound college student matches societal needs. A strong case can be made that a greater need exists in the post-Vietnam United States for skilled craftsmen and that higher or, possibly more exactly, longer education has been oversold. Inexorable laws of supply and demand may indeed prove that by further stimulating the supply of college-trained persons in the labor force, the GI Bill has helped to devalue the worth of a sheepskin, while societal needs were greater for the training of skilled craftsmen or technicians, which was not encouraged by the law.

Federal Manpower Programs

Federally supported manpower programs are another option open to veterans seeking vocational training. These received little attention as choices for veterans until President Nixon announced his veterans program in June 1971. In the past, the major thrust of manpower programs has been to train disadvantaged individuals and to assist them in finding employment. Beginning in March 1972, however, Vietnam veterans were given absolute preference in all programs, except for those limited to unemployed and low-income persons under the Economic Opportunity Act.[12] As a result, all veterans who desired training, not just the disadvantaged, could enroll in federally supported programs. The options offered to veterans in the various federally funded manpower programs are not insignificant. According to the Labor Department, almost 150,000 Vietnam veterans entered manpower programs during 1972.

Whether the "absolute" preference accorded veterans will remain rhetoric or add viable options for veterans seeking vocational training remains to be seen. Veterans were attracted to the Public Employment Program funded under the Emergency Employment Act. The Labor Department has estimated that more than 60,000 Vietnam veterans were placed in state and local jobs under this program. But these were real jobs paying established wage and salary rates. Veterans apparently

---

[12] Manpower Administration, U.S. Department of Labor, "Establishment of Absolute Preference for Enrollment for Vietnam Veterans in Manpower Training" (March 21, 1972), Manpower Administration Order no. 3–72 (mimeographed), pp. 1–2.

found the training programs less attractive. Despite the priority they received, a mere 40,000 Vietnam veterans enrolled in MDTA institutional programs during 1972, although possibly five times as many enrolled in "below college-level" training supported by the GI Bill during that year.

Although 40,000 veterans enrolled in MDTA institutional training and another 18,000 enrolled in OJT sponsored by the Labor Department, not all were able to collect GI Bill benefits. The average MDTA training stipends of almost $225 per month added to the basic GI Bill benefit of $220 each month would appear to be a substantial incentive for veterans seeking below college institutional training. However, some MDTA courses are contracted with private institutions which do not meet the VA requirement of having been in existence for two years. Federally supported OJT programs of less than six months' duration and which do not assure a reasonable certainty of providing a job also do not conform to VA standards. Some 15,000 veterans did enroll in the Labor Department's apprenticeship programs for which the standards are generally the same for that agency as well as VA.

Chapter 4.

The Disabled Veteran: A Special Case

Throughout American history, society has felt a pressing responsibility to the veteran disabled in military service. During the post-World War I period, disabled veterans were singled out for readjustment benefits. Within the decade (1920s) after the end of the war, more than 675,000 veterans applied for vocational rehabilitation, of whom half were found eligible. The VA claimed that of the 180,000 disabled veterans who eventually entered training, 129,000 successfully completed their courses. The trainees were equally distributed in institutional and OJT programs, and the remaining one-third participated in a combination of both types of training.[1]

The presumed successes of the World War I program paved the way for a similar program for later disabled veterans. It established the feasibility of vocational rehabilitation through education and training. Moreover, the accomplishments of the educational program for disabled vet-

---

[1] President's Commission on Veterans' Pensions, *The Historical Development of Veterans' Benefits in the United States,* report to the House Committee on Veterans' Affairs, 84th Cong., 2d Sess. (May 6, 1956) (Washington, D.C.: U.S. Government Printing Office, 1956), pp. 130–31.

erans were factors in the decision to provide all World War II veterans with education and training benefits.

Vocational Rehabilitation for Veterans

The vocational rehabilitation program for disabled World War II veterans began in 1943. All servicemen with a disability of 10 percent or more were eligible. And one year later education benefits for the non-disabled were approved. More than 600,000 disabled World War II veterans, or 27 percent of those with a service-connected disability, entered vocational rehabilitation. Another 400,000 disabled veterans were counseled but did not enter the program.[2] Because vocational rehabilitation study plans were subject to a continuing monitoring by a vocational counselor, it is probable that many other disabled veterans chose their own educational programs under the regular GI Bill benefits.[3]

Under a 1950 law, veterans disabled during the Korean Conflict were provided basically the same vocational rehabilitation benefits as World War II veterans. Later, in 1962, the benefits were extended to peacetime and Vietnam veterans. However, only those whose disability was rated at 30 percent or greater were covered by the law.

Administration

Every honorably discharged veteran who receives compensation for a disability may be considered for vocational rehabilitation. The Medical Policy Board in each VA regional office has the responsibility for determining the degree of the veteran's disability and his eligibility for compensation payments. As in the case of nondisabled veterans, the adjudication division must establish his entitlement for vocational rehabilitation. Unlike those for nondisabled veterans, entitlement and enrollment in vocational rehabilitation must have a particular employment objective as their goal. For those with 30 percent and greater disability ratings, the "pronounced employment handicap" necessary to gain entitlement is presumed to exist. However, the guideline is flexible

---

[2] Department of Veterans Benefits, Veterans Administration, *Record and Evaluation of the Vocational Rehabilitation Program for Service-Connected Disabled Veterans* (Washington, D.C.: U.S. Government Printing Office, 1955), printed for the use of the House Committee on Veterans' Affairs, 84th Cong., 1st Sess., p. 9.

[3] President's Commission on Veterans' Pensions, *Historical Development of Veterans' Benefits, op. cit.*, p. 133.

enough to allow the vocational counselor to deny benefits to some veterans with a greater than 30 percent disability if he determines that vocational rehabilitation is unnecessary. And he could establish eligibility for some veterans whose lesser disabilities constitute employment handicaps.

Vocational rehabilitation is denied in few cases. Of the 20,500 veterans for whom counseling was completed during 1971, only 2,560 were denied training. Most were men with a disability rating less than 30 percent. Those denied vocational rehabilitation are then assisted in entering a regular GI Bill program of studies.

When any doubt exists concerning the medical feasibility of training a severely disabled veteran, his case is referred to the regional office's Vocational Rehabilitation Board. The board, which is composed of personnel who specialize in counseling, training, and adjustment, helps in planning an integrated program of services — counseling, medical, and vocational — for the veteran.

Eligibility for most World War II veterans ended in 1956, and for peacetime veterans who served before 1962, the cut-off was 1971. Post-Korean veterans are eligible to enroll in vocational rehabilitation during the nine years following their release from active duty. However, extensions up to four years are possible if medical problems have delayed the beginning of training, if compensable disability was not established within the normal time period, or if a dishonorable discharge was subsequently changed, establishing the veteran's eligibility. During 1972, only 1,200 World War II and Korean veterans were among the 31,600 vocational rehabilitation trainees. Disabled Vietnam veterans accounted for 24,800 participants. During their nine- or 13-year period of eligibility, veterans are normally limited to four years of vocational rehabilitation, although exceptions can be made to lengthen the program for men whose health deteriorates or who need several different types of training at different times.

Outreach and Intake

The VA attempts to locate disabled veterans and motivate them to enroll in vocational rehabilitation as early as possible. Both the military and VA hospitals have psychologists available to counsel disabled patients. In addition, VA counselors from the regional offices visit these hospitals to begin the process of determining an education or training plan for the disabled serviceman or veteran. Those men who are not reached while in the hospital are contacted after applying for disability compensation. Copies of all disability ratings are passed on to vocational rehabilitation counselors who contact the veterans to offer VA services.

During the course of counseling and establishing an education or training plan, disabled veterans receive more intensive attention than those applying for regular GI Bill benefits. Aptitude and interest tests are normally administered along with motor ability tests to assure that a suitable occupation is chosen and that any additional physical restoration required is undertaken.

To assure as complete a coverage as possible of those disabled veterans eligible for VA benefits, the VA staff cooperates with the state vocational rehabilitation agencies. When a veteran eligible for VA benefits approaches a state agency for assistance, he is referred to the VA in order to exhaust VA services and his vocational rehabilitation entitlement before turning to the state agency for help. Although it is not frequently necessary, the VA can work with state agencies on behalf of veterans who reach the end of their nine- or 13-year period of eligibility without completing their rehabilitation to assure that the federal-state agencies will continue to aid the victims for the remainder of their programs. Other disabled veterans who are not entitled to VA vocational rehabilitation — for example, those with no service-connected handicaps — are referred to the state agency where they can receive assistance.

Benefits

Unlike the nondisabled veteran who receives only a stipend during his period of training, the costs of training and educating the disabled veteran are fully covered by the government. In addition, the veteran receives a subsistence allowance during his rehabilitation and for two months after completion (Table 8). Between 1970 and 1972 the basic benefit to an unmarried veteran in vocational rehabilitation was $135 per month. The 26 percent increase which became effective in October 1972 was comparable to other increases for nondisabled veterans, except for veterans pursuing vocational rehabilitation in OJT.

Hospitalized servicemen who enter vocational rehabilitation before they are discharged are ineligible for subsistence allowances. The stipend plus the wages of a disabled veteran in OJT is limited to the base pay of

TABLE 8

Disabled Veterans Receive Monthly Subsistence Allowances
in Addition to Training Costs

	Dependents			For Each Additional Dependent
Category	None	One	Two	
Institutional:				
Full time	$170	$211	$248	$18
Three-quarter time	128	159	187	14
Half time	85	106	124	9
Farm, apprenticeship, or other on-the-job training, full time	$148	$179	$207	$14

Source: VIETNAM ERA VETERANS' READJUSTMENT ASSISTANCE ACT OF 1972 (October 24, 1972), Public Law 92-540.

a fully trained journeyman. When the trainee's total income exceeds that amount, his stipend is cut accordingly.

The veteran qualifying for vocational rehabilitation is not likely to get rich while participating in the program, but the financial benefits appear adequate to maintain the veteran until he can work again. Since most are qualified for at least a 30 percent disability compensation, the combined monthly income under the 1972 law for an unmarried veteran in an institutional program was $247, none of which had to be applied to the costs of training. Tuition, fees, books, supplies, and equipment that are necessary for the program of study are covered by VA funds. A disabled veteran enrolled in OJT receives a total of $225 in compensation and stipends plus whatever wages he earned.

Disabled Veterans in Training

Since the beginning of the vocational rehabilitation program in 1918, more than 900,000 disabled veterans have entered training as follows:

Time period	*Number*
World War I	180,000
World War II	621,000
Korean Conflict	77,000
Post-Korean peacetime	24,000
Vietnam War	44,000

Data from the first five years of the Vietnam era show that the typical disabled veteran in a vocational rehabilitation program was under 30 years of age, had at least one dependent, and had at least a high school education. As was true of his predecessor from World War II and the Korean Conflict, his disability was likely due to an orthopedic problem or a mental disorder. In only 14 percent of the cases was impairment less than 30 percent. Almost four of 10 vocational rehabilitation enrollees had disabilities rated at 30 or 40 percent, and another two of 10 were totally disabled.[4]

Disabled veterans normally receive their training in the same institutions, OJT sites, and farm courses as the nondisabled. Like other veterans, a greater proportion of disabled Vietnam veterans has turned to colleges and universities than disabled veterans from previous periods (Table 9). Six of 10 disabled Vietnam veterans chose to undertake vocational rehabilitation in college, compared with approximately one-fourth of the World War II and one-third of the Korean disabled veterans.

The institutional courses in which disabled veterans have enrolled during the post-Korean period vary greatly. College programs in education, administrative specialties, and managerial skills were most popular. Below college institutional trainees frequently have chosen employment goals in such professional and technical fields as administration, drafting, and technical occupations, in clerical and sales work, or in such trade and industrial occupations as mechanics, repairmen, and assemblers.[5]

The decline in the proportion of veterans enrolling in OJT has been even more dramatic among those in vocational rehabilitation programs than among regular GI Bill trainees. After World War II, more than one-third of the vocational rehabilitation trainees were training on-site, compared with only 5 percent of Vietnam era trainees.

Counseling

Since counseling on a career choice is an integral part of the vocational rehabilitation process, it can only be concluded that more disabled veterans are seeking and being encouraged to choose institutional courses which lead to professional, technical, and managerial types of jobs.

---

[4] Department of Veterans Benefits, Veterans Administration (February 14, 1972) (unpublished material).

[5] Veterans Administration, "Programs of a Study of Peacetime Disabled Veterans, January 1963 through November 30, 1970" (mimeographed).

TABLE 9

More Disabled Vietnam Veterans Enrolled in College-Level Training by June 1972
Than Those from Previous Periods

Program of Study	World War II		Korean Conflict		Post-Korean Conflict		Vietnam War	
	Total Enrolled	Percentage of Total	Total Enrolled	Percentage of Total	Total Enrolled	Percentage of Total	Total Enrolled	Percentage of Total
Disabled veterans	621,000		77,000		24,000		44,000	
Percentage enrolled:								
College		24.6%		32.2%		43.8%		61.9%
Less than college		24.8		47.3		49.9		32.7
On-the-job training		38.3		16.2		5.7		5.0
Farm		12.3%		4.3%		0.6%		0.4%

Source: Department of Veterans Benefits, Veterans Administration, *Veterans Benefits under Current Educational Programs* (June 1972), Information Bulletin no. 24-72-6, p. 35.

Most of the disabled OJT trainees are working at trade and industrial jobs, where on-site training predominates. The sites, however, are usually in small businesses or shops or in the government, where special work conditions can more readily be adapted for the veteran.

Special Services

Because the emphasis is to ensure that disabled veterans receive a complete vocational rehabilitation program, special programs have been developed for severely disabled veterans whose handicaps prevent them from beginning an institutional or regular OJT program immediately. These special services include special restorative training, remedial education, placement in sheltered workshops, and homebound training. During fiscal year 1971, approximately 800 disabled veterans were in these programs.

Special adjustment programs, such as mobility training or braille lessons, are provided where possible by the VA Department of Medicine and Surgery, although other special rehabilitation facilities outside the VA can be used. Remedial education is provided to those disabled veterans who need it in order to enter a trade, technical, or college program.

Some disabled veterans in need of a protective setting as a transition to a normal work site are placed in sheltered workshops. Licensed by the Labor Department, these public and private workshops are not required to meet VA OJT requirements. Goodwill Industries, where employees repair items for resale, is a typical sheltered workshop. Although in some cases sheltered workshops provide extended or terminal employment, the VA attempts to place disabled veterans there only until their self-confidence and skills have improved sufficiently for them to move on to OJT or institutional training. None of these types of special restorative training is considered a vocational rehabilitation program by itself. It is only an added step to ensure that the disabled veteran will successfully complete his training or education and be placed in a permanent job.

Homebound Training

Another special program is homebound training for severely disabled but intellectually capable veterans who can undertake a training course only in their homes. Not only medical obstacles but motivational problems must be overcome in the case of a homebound veteran. Training is conducted for these men so long as it is medically feasible. Most often the homebound veteran who takes vocational rehabilitation develops a skilled trade or profession, such as repair work or accounting, which he can develop into a small business. During 1971, 250 homebound veterans were being trained.

Participation in Vocational Rehabilitation

As of June 30, 1972, there were 308,800 disabled Vietnam veterans receiving disability compensation, of whom 137,000 had a 30 percent or greater disability, the usual cutoff point for eligibility. However, not all of the 44,000 disabled Vietnam era veterans who had entered vocational rehabilitation were classified disabled 30 percent or greater. The participation rate in vocational rehabilitation as of mid-1972 was therefore less than 30 percent, somewhat lower than among the nondisabled GI Bill trainees. It may not be meaningful to compare participation rates of the groups, since little is known about the total need for rehabilitation among the disabled or their ability to participate. Many of the lesser disabled may not require vocational training but need only help in finding a job. Also, there may be some among the 23,000 who are 100 percent disabled and cannot participate.

More important in measuring the success of the vocational rehabilitation program is the proportion of men who take vocational rehabilitation and are rehabilitated. Since follow-up studies are not available, the only measure provided by the VA is the proportion of the World War II and Korean Conflict trainees who completed their program of education or training and were placed in jobs for which they were trained. According to this criterion, 61 percent were rehabilitated.[6] Not included among the rehabilitated are those who dropped out of the program to accept jobs. Because so many post-Korean disabled veterans are still in training, it is difficult to estimate how many will be totally rehabilitated. During fiscal year 1971, there were 4,280 disabled veterans who had completed training; 90 percent of them found jobs in the fields for which they were trained.

Some problems do exist, however, among those enrolled in vocational rehabilitation. Although some 31,600 disabled veterans were enrolled in a vocational rehabilitation program during fiscal year 1972,

---

[6] Veterans Administration, "Rehabilitation Rates: Vocational Rehabilitation Trainees" (unpublished material), includes those World War II and Korean Conflict veterans who entered training through June 30, 1971.

only 20,800 were in training in April, the peak month of the school year. Part of the difference may be due to the exit of some rehabilitated veterans. Other disabled veterans who locate employment opportunities while in training prefer to take advantage of the security of a job and abandon their training. They are not counted as rehabilitated. Others are rehospitalized and must drop out of training. Those who drop out, regardless of the reason, must apply for a redetermination of their entitlement before they can reenter the rehabilitation program.

Cost of Vocational Rehabilitation

World War I vocational rehabilitation is estimated to have cost $645 million. The comparable bill for World War II to June 1971 has totaled $421 million, coupled with more than $1.5 billion in subsistence allowances.

At an average cost of about $2,000 per enrollee, the total direct cost of the veterans vocational rehabilitation program during fiscal year 1972 was more than $60 million. Subsistence allowances averaged $1,300 per trainee, and the remainder was allocated to the cost of training. These direct costs, however, represent only the most visible part of the expenditures to readjust disabled veterans to civilian life. The VA has apparently never attempted to analyze the indirect costs of the program. Medical expenditures and compensation payments for disabled veterans, although not defined as readjustment outlays, are necessary expenditures to guaranty that the disabled veteran is restored to a complete life.

To support the vocational rehabilitation program, for example, the VA supports some 280 counseling psychologists and 180 vocational rehabilitation specialists in its regional offices. The total cost of payroll and overhead (including support staff) amounted probably to $20,000 per employee, or another $9.6 million to the vocational rehabilitation bill.

The special restorative programs and remedial education, in which some 400 disabled veterans were enrolled during 1971, are additional costs incurred before the veterans formally begin their vocational rehabilitation. No estimates of the cost of these programs are available. Hospitalization, medical care, and prostheses necessary to complete their training are available to vocational rehabilitation participants whether or not they would be authorized under VA regulations. The medical expenses for restorative programs and for medical care for the disabled while in training are included in the Department of Medicine and Surgery budget and are not computed separately for vocational rehabilitation trainees. Remedial education is also not listed as a separate expense.

Additional minor assistance is also offered. For example, the VA maintains a revolving loan fund for disabled veterans in vocational rehabilitation. Until October 1972 a trainee could borrow up to $100 as an "advance" to be repaid interest-free; the amount was increased to $200 under the 1972 law. During 1971, some $351,056 was borrowed from the fund, and $343,112 was repaid to it.

Other Readjustment Benefits for the Disabled

Although not related directly to the costs of rehabilitation, several other substantial forms of readjustment assistance are accorded disabled veterans. Under a program established in 1946, veterans receiving compensation for loss of a hand or foot or serious impairment of vision are eligible to receive assistance in purchasing an automobile or other conveyance together with necessary adaptive equipment. As of January 1971, the basic allowance was raised from $1,600 to $2,800 for purchase of the vehicle and the installation, maintenance, repair, and replacement of the adaptive equipment. As of June 1971, more than 62,000 disabled veterans had taken advantage of the program, at a cost of $101.2 million. Moreover, since 1948 paraplegic veterans have received assistance in obtaining suitable housing, including any special facilities that the nature of their disabilities requires. The maximum amount of the grant was raised from $12,500 to $17,500, effective July 1972. It can be used to cover up to 50 percent of the cost of land and construction. By June 1972 more than 12,000 such grants had been made, at a cost of $120.7 million.

Readjustment benefits for disabled veterans extend beyond the VA. While the VA's vocational rehabilitation specialists are responsible for following the vocational rehabilitation trainee through his program of studies, culminating with helping to place him in a job, the specialists depend heavily upon the placement offices of the training institutions, the U.S. Employment Service, and the Civil Service Commission for help. While the Employment Service has traditionally given preference to veterans, the disabled receive top priority under the law. The Civil

Service Commission gives the disabled veteran an additional 10 points on his examination score (instead of the five points for other veterans).

In all federal manpower programs in which veterans have priority in enrolling, disabled veterans are to be the first selected. Finally, disabled veterans, seeking to exercise their reemployment rights and not qualified to perform their former duties because of their disabilities, are entitled to another position in the same company that will provide them similar seniority, status, and pay.

The disabled veteran is considered by the VA to be a special case most worthy of extra help and attention. One VA official stated that "the Congress has never refused anything for direct benefits; there are no budget constraints" and added that the VA is not "even told to take only 'calculated risks' in attempting the vocational rehabilitation of disabled veterans." As for the indirect costs of the program for the VA and the expenditures by the state social rehabilitation services, the U.S. Employment Service, and the Civil Service Commission, it is safe to conclude that all reasonable efforts are made to restore the disabled veteran's employability.

Drug-Dependent Veterans

While the nation has long assumed the responsibility to provide intensive services to physically and mentally handicapped veterans, the recent concern regarding drug usage by servicemen and veterans has raised demands that the military and the VA treat drug dependency as a disability. The VA has provided special assistance to alcoholic veterans since 1969. However, alcohol abuse and its treatment have not generated the same controversy as that surrounding young soldiers who chose to alter consciousness with injected or ingested drugs as opposed to imbibed ones.

Contrary to some persuasive evidence that drug abuse among veterans may be service connected, if not service induced, the VA continues to treat drug dependence in much the same manner as alcoholism — as a nonservice-connected social problem. GAO found, for example, that drugs have been readily and cheaply available to servicemen in Vietnam.[7] Expanding on the problem, the Harris study[8] found that veterans

---

[7] U.S. General Accounting Office, *Drug Abuse Control Program Activities in Vietnam* (August 11, 1972), no. B-164031(2), enclosure B, pp. 1–2.

[8] Louis Harris and Associates, Inc., *A Study of the Problems Facing Vietnam Era Veterans on Their Readjustment to Civilian Life* (Washington, D.C.: U.S. Govern-

as well as the public believed that the pressure of war, homesickness, boredom, and the easy availability of drugs account for much of the veterans' drug problem. Whatever the reason for drug use among military personnel, the proportion of those who use drugs while in the military was almost double the percentage who had experimented with drugs in civilian life. The study observed that it would be a legitimate conclusion to call the military "a breeder of drug use."

Estimates of the extent of drug use among servicemen and veterans vary widely. Dr. Jerome Jaffe, Director of the Special Action Office for Drug Abuse Prevention, reported that between 4 and 5 percent of those soldiers screened by urinalysis tests showed positive results. The Harris study reported that only 2 percent of Vietnam veterans were heroin addicts upon their return to civilian life. While the Special Action Office for Drug Abuse Prevention estimated that there are approximately 100,000 veterans of all ages who are addicts among the 500,000 to 750,000 drug-addicted Americans, the VA estimated the number at 60,000 veterans.

The VA extended the classification "service-connected disability" to venereal disease, but drug abuse and alcoholism remain nonservice connected. If either were to become compensable, the VA would be required to provide not only hospitalization and compensation, but also vocational rehabilitation services to those affected. Instead the VA has unofficially treated the veteran addict as a special case and provided him services not actually required by law and not available generally to veterans with nonservice-connected medical problems. While most veterans ostensibly must meet a "needs" test to be eligible for VA treatment, veteran addicts are generally admitted for drug treatment with little regard to financial need. Proposals that VA drug treatment be made available to veterans regardless of their discharge status have been opposed as inequitable by the VA and the veterans lobby, since veterans discharged under less than honorable conditions are excluded from VA care, even if they have a service-connected disability.

To help extend the VA services to those with other than honorable discharges, the Secretary of Defense ordered in August 1971 that discharges solely for drug offenses be reviewed upon request of the veteran

---

ment Printing Office, 1972), printed for the use of the Senate Committee on Veterans' Affairs, 92d Cong., 2d Sess., pp. 169–70.

and changed to administrative discharges "under honorable conditions."
While administrative discharges for drug abuse rose from 5,000 to 9,000
between 1970 and 1971, the proportion of undesirable discharges solely
for drug usage fell as the Armed Services began "exemption programs"
during mid-1971 for drug abusers who voluntarily requested assistance.
Under these programs men could ask for medical help for their drug
problems without risking court martial or discharge under less than
honorable conditions. GAO reported that the success of the programs is
limited because soldiers who use drugs and the Defense Department dis-
trust each other.[9]

During 1971, more than 16,000 drug abusers voluntarily asked for
treatment under the exemption programs; 9,000 other drug users were
identified through law-enforcement activities. In June 1971, urinalysis
testing for servicemen in Vietnam began. When a soldier is identified as
a drug user, he is normally sent to an Armed Services detoxification center for three to 14 days, and some are referred to VA drug treatment
facilities for continued assistance.[10]

In January 1971, the VA opened its first five drug-dependence treatment centers, and by June 1972, 44 such centers had been established
involving 52 VA facilities and two satellite clinics outside VA facilities.
More than 11,000 veterans were admitted to VA facilities with drug-
dependence problems during 1971; another 8,800 veterans and 2,700
servicemen were admitted to such facilities during the first six months of
1972. The eventual cost per veteran for a full three years of treatment
was estimated at $4,750.[11]

Four of every 10 drug patients continued with outpatient treatment
upon discharge from the VA hospitals. Of the 6,000 veterans who left
outpatient care between January 1971 and June 1972, some 1,900 were
rehospitalized, and 1,600 terminated the program. While the latter
group is probably the most accurate estimate of those who successfully

---

9 U.S. General Accounting Office, *Drug Abuse Control Activities Affecting Military Personnel* (August 11, 1972), no. B-164031(2), pp. 20, 30, 40–41.

10 House Committee on Veterans' Affairs, "Veterans Administration Drug Dependence Program" (Washington, D.C.: U.S. Government Printing Office, June
1972), p. 1.

11 Senate Subcommittee on Health and Hospitals, Committee on Veterans'
Affairs, and Subcommittee on Alcoholism and Narcotics, Committee on Labor and
Public Welfare, 92d Cong., 1st Sess., "Hearings on Drug Addiction and Abuse among
Military Veterans" (June 23, 1971) (Washington, D.C.: U.S. Government Printing
Office, 1971), part 1, pp. 135, 173.

completed treatment, the rehabilitation criteria for the drug-dependent veteran are not well defined. In light of the VA's original estimate that a successful rehabilitation program would require three to six weeks of hospitalization and then approximately 70 outpatient visits each year for as long as three years, it may be assumed that a significant proportion of drug patients leave the program before they are successfully rehabilitated.

VA Administrator Donald Johnson noted that satisfactory job placement would be one measure of successful rehabilitation for the addict. The VA has arranged for at least one vocational counselor to be assigned to each of the drug treatment facilities to aid drug abusers in making the transition from medical care to school, training, or employment. The VA has opposed legislation that would formally extend its vocational rehabilitation program to veteran addicts. Instead the drug program relies on medical care for the drug-dependent veteran, combined with education and training under the regular GI Bill . . . as if the veteran had experienced no disabling problem.

Chapter 5.

Housing and Other Loans to Veterans

The GI Bill offers assistance to veterans to purchase homes and farms. This aid might be differentiated from the other direct benefits as "deferred readjustment" because few veterans take advantage of the housing loan program shortly after they leave the Armed Forces. The program dates back to the 1944 GI Bill which established a program of guarantied, insured, and direct loans to veterans to purchase or improve a home or farm or to finance a business. Similar loan programs were extended to Korean veterans. The home loan guaranty attracted the largest proportion of veterans and has been the nucleus of the program since its inception. When VA loan benefits were extended to post-Korean veterans in 1966, only home and farm loans were included in the program for these veterans.

Although the VA loan program was originally intended to be an aid in the veterans' readjustment from military to civilian life, the 1970 law which eliminated the termination dates for eligibility has rendered the program a permanent veterans' benefit. As of mid-1972, approximately 38 percent of eligible World War II veterans and 44 percent of eligible

Korean veterans had participated in the loan program. Normally, a veteran does not turn to the VA for loan assistance until several years after his release from active duty — until he finishes school, locates a job, and marries. Thus, only 10 percent of the post-Korean veterans had used the program as of June 1972. Some 20 million veterans or their dependents remain eligible for loan benefits over and above the 8.5 million veterans who have taken part in one of the loan programs.

GUARANTIED OR INSURED LOANS

Veterans who desire to purchase homes can make arrangements with the lender of their choice. The VA guaranties 60 percent of the home loan or $12,500, whichever is less, against default. The extent of the guaranty declines as the loan is repaid, since the VA guaranty is a fixed percentage of the outstanding amount of the loan. The maximum rate of interest is set by the VA to be competitive with the market rate. It cannot exceed the Federal Housing Administration (FHA) rate but is normally equal to it. The VA also contracts with private appraisers to determine the reasonable value of the property, above which no guaranty coverage will be extended. (The veteran may pay more than the reasonable value if he pays in cash.)

Guaranties on business real estate and on nonreal estate, for which World War II and Korean veterans remain eligible, cover up to either 50 percent of the loan or up to $4,000 on real estate or $2,000 on other purchases. Only 3 percent of the loan guaranties undertaken by the VA as of the end of fiscal year 1972 were business loans. Since the law was never updated to allow competitive rates of interest and larger loans, the VA business loan program is no longer attractive to veterans or to lenders.

Veteran farmers are eligible for two types of farm loan guaranties. The first, a farm-residence loan, parallels the home loan guaranty program. The second is a guaranteed loan to purchase or improve land, livestock, equipment, or stock in a cooperative. The guaranty limits are the same as on business loans. Since the amounts of the farm-business loans are small, it is not surprising that few such loans are guarantied each year. A more important program for veteran farmers is the loan service of the Farmers Home Administration of the U.S. Department of Agriculture, which provides loans to purchase real estate and for operating expenses. Veterans receive preference where funds are limited under this program and priority in the processing of their applications.

As of the end of fiscal year 1972, 8.1 million guaranteed or insured loans had been made with a VA initial liability of $46.8 billion on loans totaling $90.2 billion. More than 95 percent of the loans were for homes (Table 10). In 1971 the average VA-guarantied home loan recipient had a monthly income of $733 after taxes, of which he paid $241 for housing expenses — repayment on his loan plus taxes, insurance, and maintenance. The average purchase price of a new house was $25,100 and of an existing home, 21,400. More than seven of 10 home buyers made no down payment and nine of 10 negotiated mortgages of 25 to 30 years.[1]

DIRECT LOAN PROGRAM

The VA also administers a direct loan program for veterans who are unable to arrange a private loan due to shortage of housing credit in their area. A veteran may only use a direct loan to purchase, improve, or refinance a home or farmhouse. The maximum loan is generally

TABLE 10

Most VA Loan Activity Involves Homes for Veterans
(Cumulative to June 30, 1972)

Kind of Loan	Number of Loans (thousands)	Amount (billions)
Guarantied or insured:		
Home	7,841	$89.2
Farm	71	0.3
Business	229	0.7
Total	8,141	90.2
Direct loans	314	3.0
Total — all loans	8,455	$93.2

Source: Loan Guaranty Service, Veterans Administration (June 20, 1972) (unpublished data).

[1] U.S. Bureau of the Census, *Statistical Abstract of the United States, 1972* (Washington, D.C.: U.S. Government Printing Office, 1972), p. 693.

$21,000, except in high-cost areas where $25,000 is the limit. The amount is reduced for veterans who have used a portion of their entitlement for a guarantied loan.

The VA acts as the lender in the case of direct loans. As in the case of guarantied loans, rate and reasonable value of the property are set by the VA. Direct loans which are sold to private investors (about one-fifth of the direct loans made or one-fourth of the funds loaned) are sold with a guaranty; in the case of default, the claim and property acquisition costs are paid out of the loan guaranty fund.[2]

THE HOUSING SUBSIDY

In line with VA concern for the well-being of its clients, VA regulations afford lenders broad discretion in extending or redesigning the terms of the loan to allow the borrower to retain his property if he faces default. Nevertheless, defaults do occur, and the VA consequently becomes involved in acquiring and selling property. When a guarantied loan is foreclosed, the lender has the option of reselling the property or, as is done in most cases, of conveying it to the VA. In the case of direct loans, the property title is conveyed directly to the VA. The VA in turn normally resells its properties through local real estate brokers, although in some instances buyers can finance the property purchase with the VA. As of the end of fiscal year 1972, more than 270,000 home loans, or 3.5 percent of the 7.8 million home loans guarantied since 1944, were foreclosed and claims paid by the VA.

The low rate of foreclosure under the VA home loan programs, combined with similar successes in the FHA programs, has acted as a liberalizing influence on mortgage practices. According to one authoritative estimate, approximately $1 billion annually in benefits accrue to participants in these loan programs (due mainly to tax savings by the mortgagees).[3]

VA loan guaranties and direct loans are made to veterans who meet the qualifications of sound income and satisfactory credit rating necessary in the market for mortgage funds. The low-income veteran seeking

---

[2] House Subcommittee on HUD-Space-Science-Veterans, Committee on Appropriations, 92d Cong., 2d Sess. (March 20, 1972), "Hearings on HUD-Space-Science-Veterans Appropriations for 1973" (Washington, D.C.: U.S. Government Printing Office, 1972), part 2, p. 962.

[3] Henry J. Aaron, *Shelter and Subsidies* (Washington, D.C.: The Brookings Institution, 1972), pp. 84–85, 89.

housing assistance must turn to the FHA on the same terms as non-veterans. Rent supplements and public housing programs are designed to offer preferences to low-income families, the handicapped, and the elderly, and do not extend preferences on the basis of veteran status alone.

The VA loan program raises two issues for the study of the veterans' welfare system. First, what advantage does the VA program offer to ex-servicemen not available to the remainder of the population? Also, to what extent is the program subsidized by the U.S. treasury?

FHA loan insurance parallels the VA home loan program. A comparison of the terms of FHA and VA loans for single-family, owner-occupied homes demonstrates the basic similarities of the two programs. Both VA guaranties and FHA insurance allow a 30-year repayment plan on any standard amortizing schedule established by the lender. Neither loan involves a prepayment penalty. However, the VA home loan guaranty has two significant advantages. First, the FHA insures home loans up to $33,000, for which the home buyer pays an additional 0.5 percent interest on his loan. The VA loan guaranty involves no additional interest charge over the base rate. Since 1966, the VA has been allowed to set interest rates competitive with FHA rates. Previously, the maximum allowable VA rate was set by Congress, which did not act as quickly as necessary to respond to changes in market conditions. The second advantage for the veteran is the difference in down payment under the VA and FHA programs. So long as the veteran's loan is for the reasonable value of the home established by the VA, he is not required to make a down payment, unless of course the lender demands one. Regular FHA standards allow loan insurance to cover 97 percent of the first $15,000 of the value of the loan, 90 percent of the next $10,000, and 80 percent of any amount over $25,000. Thus a veteran purchasing a $30,000 home at 7 percent on a 30-year term would make no down payment and would pay $199.60 per month in principal and interest, while a nonveteran buying the same home with FHA insurance would be required to make a down payment of $2,450 and would pay $204.29 monthly.[4] Thus the veteran would save more than $4,000 over the life of the mortgage.

---

[4] William S. Mussenden (ed.), *The Homeowner's Guide* (Washington, D.C.: The Homeowner's Guide, Inc., 1971), pp. 23–27.

As a result of the differences in interest rates and down payments, the VA and FHA housing programs have income redistribution and transfer implications. While the 0.5 percent additional charge to FHA participants redistributes income from higher income home buyers (who are lower risks) to low-income participants (who are greater risks), the VA program involves no redistribution of income among participants. Instead the VA guaranties are largely income transfers to the predominantly middle-income veterans who participate. Moreover, because VA loan guaranties are more likely to cover loans near 100 percent of the value of the home, even at higher income levels, than the FHA insurance, income transfers to veterans are larger.[5]

Both the VA loan guaranty and the direct loan program are operated from revolving funds. Although the primary goal of the VA housing program is to provide viable credit assistance to veterans, among the secondary goals is the management of financing, avoiding congressional appropriations and losses to the government. Before 1962, the loan guaranty program was financed directly by appropriations, and receipts were deposited in the general fund of the U.S. treasury. Appropriations for the guaranty program totaled $730 million between 1944 and 1962. A loan guaranty revolving fund was established in 1962 and as of the end of fiscal year 1972 had a net loss of $100 million. The only appropriations made since the inception of the revolving funds have been to meet shortages in the sale of participation certificates, accounting by the end of 1972 to $18.6 million. These instruments were sold when high discount rates prevented the sale of entire loans. Conversely, the direct loan fund which had been in operation since 1950 enjoyed a $251.3 million surplus. This fund borrows from the U.S. treasury at its loan rate and then lends the money to veterans at a higher rate. An additional $472 million was spent on administrative expenses since the VA loan program began — a little more than $50 per loan. Thus the net cost of the VA housing program at the end of fiscal year 1972 was $320.4 million.[6] This does not include the $120.4 million paid for special adaptive housing for disabled veterans, which is also administered by the loan guaranty personnel. Considering the services performed by the VA and the

---

[5] Henry J. Aaron, *Shelter and Subsidies, op. cit.,* pp. 88–89.

[6] House Subcommittee on HUD-Space-Science-Veterans, "HUD-Space-Science-Veterans," *op. cit.,* p. 856.

benefits accruing to those veterans who participate, the costs of the home loan program have been reasonable.

Although the loan guaranty program may not appeal to Vietnam veterans immediately upon their return home, it will most likely result in considerable savings to those men who eventually settle down to a job, a family, and a home. But unlike the federally supported FHA program which charges a fee to home buyers, the VA loan guaranty is free to veterans. Since the government assumes the risk without receiving compensation from the veterans, the VA loan program is another example of a publicly subsidized program whose benefits can accrue only to veterans.

Chapter 6.

Assessment and Future Direction

The Vietnam veterans who have returned to civilian life have faced a variety of social and economic problems, the most important of which have been locating jobs and embarking on renewing a program of education. Many were too young to acquire a skill or profession before entering the service and were trained for combat duty in the service; few had learned a salable skill while in the Armed Forces. Since 1969, they have had to compete for jobs in a recession or high-unemployment economy, and the high price of education did not always make the return to school an attractive choice.

The readjustment kit provided to their predecessors from earlier wars has been refined and expanded to offer Vietnam veterans a wide range of benefits in employment and education to suit individual preferences. But despite the sustained efforts by the VA and other federal agencies to inform them of their options, many veterans were not helped by the readjustment programs. While 1972 increases in GI Bill stipends may encourage some of the job seekers to enter school or training programs, the individual veteran's job search will continue to be his most

important readjustment problem. At the same time, employment programs for veterans remain the weakest tool in the readjustment kit, so
long as job shortages prevail in the economy.

Job creation and employment services for veterans have relied
largely upon rhetoric. While the public employment service maintains
a priority for veterans seeking jobs, it has traditionally listed a limited
number of jobs, and relatively few veterans received substantial assistance through its services. President Nixon's directive to the Employment Service to expand job opportunities for veterans added little real
help. The anticipated 1.2 million job orders from federal government
contractors failed to materialize, and it is doubtful whether the National
Alliance for Businessmen's much ballyhooed pledge of 100,000 jobs for
veterans created a significant number of jobs . . . except in corporate
press releases.

On the other hand, priority for veterans in federal employment and
job creation programs during a period of high unemployment in the
economy discriminated against other disadvantaged individuals who
may have required equal or greater services. Veterans who filled the
Public Employment Program's jobs during 1972 were largely white,
high school graduates, with less than three of 10 being classified as "disadvantaged." While establishing such priorities was politically expedi-
ent, it may not have been equitable. Despite the outreach efforts undertaken by the VA to attract more GI Bill trainees, no attempt was ever
made to determine who the millions of veterans were who did not choose
education or training assistance, nor was it determined which services
they might require.

For veterans who chose to return to school or training, the VA is the
largest single source of readjustment assistance. However, little is known
about the effectiveness of the VA programs. Follow-up of GI Bill trainees
is nonexistent. The VA apparently considers its mandate completed
once the veteran exhausts eligibility or leaves the program for any other
reason.

For disabled veterans, whose programs of study are more closely
monitored, the agency keeps score of those rehabilitated but does no
follow-up to determine whether they continue to advance in employment. All disabled veterans who complete their course of training or
education are automatically counted among the "rehabilitated." It is

significant, however, to stress that the VA does not restrict participation in the rehabilitation program to potential success cases. On the contrary, the more disabled the veteran, the greater the interest of the VA in helping him.

In the absence of follow-up data on the impact of readjustment programs on participating veterans, no clear determination can be made of whether the taxpayers' money is being invested wisely. For example, the widespread enrollment by a large proportion of veterans using GI Bill benefits in correspondence courses offers room to question the effectiveness of the readjustment program. Follow-up information from GAO on those veterans who failed to complete correspondence training tended to support the speculation that those courses are a waste of the veterans' time and the public's money. Many veterans are lured into correspondence programs under false pretenses and fail to learn a useful skill.

VA educational programs are inherently biased in favor of higher education. A college student receives his full-time training stipend for 14 credit hours per week, while the veteran enrolled in below college technical or vocational schools must attend at least 25 hours per week of training. Moreover, a college student can change his career goal several times in the course of completing his four-year degree. Veterans in vocational and OJT programs cannot switch their occupational objective as freely.

There is no argument that individuals should have a free choice of which types of training and education to pursue or that the VA provides the veteran such an opportunity to select his own program of study. Moreover, the GI Bill is used by many to acquire a higher education that they otherwise might not have obtained. According to one estimate about one-fourth of the post-World War II college education undertaken by veterans would not have been completed without the help of the GI Bill.[1] While providing those men with the chance to realize their highest potential is a worthy social goal, it raises questions regarding the desirability of providing preference to veterans in education and, within that preference, of encouraging more and more veterans to choose college-level programs. First, the government does not offer other

---

[1] Thrainn Eggertsson, *Economic Aspects of Higher Education Taken under the World War II GI Bill of Rights* (Columbus, Ohio: Research Foundation, Ohio State University, 1972), p. 145.

individuals in the society equal incentives to continue their education . . .
this conflicts with the principles of equity. The second, more crucial
issue is whether the government should induce veterans to pursue programs of higher education while both society and the individual may
benefit from an expansion of the supply of craftsmen and individuals
with skilled trades.

Nevertheless, the veterans' readjustment kit has aided millions of
veterans in recouping the losses incurred while they served and in ful-
filling their career objectives. Preferential laws made it possible for
many veterans, particularly blacks, to gain employment in public jobs.
More than four of every 10 eligible veterans have received education
or training benefits, and 8.5 million received loan assistance from the
VA. Among these men who were uprooted from civilian society, the continuing popularity of the programs attests to such programs' successes.

The VA operates efficiently in delivering services to returning veterans and makes the programs easily available. While decentralization
of services has yet to be achieved in many federal social programs, the
VA has served its clients from 57 regional offices, each fully staffed to
provide the range of programs available. More recently, the U.S. veterans assistance centers and counseling on military bases have expanded
this effort. Even in sparsely populated areas, information on veterans'
benefits is only a telephone call away, and that is sometimes provided
free. Few activities of the Department of Health, Education and Welfare or the Labor Department can be said to have such a successful outreach organization. Moreover, the VA operates with a relatively small
administrative staff and enjoys much private volunteer support from
veterans organizations and other private groups.

Despite these efforts, the VA outreach has failed to motivate some of
the most needy. More attention must be given to the problems of those
who do not respond. While the 1970 amendments to the veterans law
included special education provisions for the disadvantaged, participation rates for the deficiently educated still lag behind the others.

Other changes in the present system of readjustment benefits would
increase their impact on those served. Until the fall of 1972, the unemployment rate of veterans remained higher than that of nonveterans,
despite a variety of public and private efforts to locate jobs and to encourage employers to treat veterans preferentially. Whether the recent

improvement in their unemployment situation is due to a gathering momentum in the employment programs or the coincidental economic upturn is uncertain. But the improvement does not eliminate the need for more attention to the transitional problems in moving from military to civilian employment.

Education and training stipends are too often paid automatically to veterans who waste time in correspondence courses or unproductive college classes. Correspondence enrollment should be curtailed when more productive education and training programs are available. Greater incentives should be offered to those in skills training to render it equal to college study. Counseling on career objectives should be given greater priority. VA services are delivered with maximum respect for the individual and few bureaucratic delays. Concern is for providing the most generous help short of waste, not the least aid sufficient to sustain. The readjustment of disabled veterans is perhaps the most outstanding example of this policy.

Without the stout support of Congress and the public, the VA no doubt would not be as effective. Problems in the delivery of services have been quickly corrected by legislative and administrative changes. Lags in the payment of education benefits, which constituted one administrative hurdle for veteran students at the beginning of each semester, were bridged by the adoption of an early payment plan. Agreement in Congress on the continuing increases in the level of education benefits to match rising costs of education may not have been unanimous, but most differences occurred on the size of the increase, not the increase itself. Congress was also sensitive to the desirability to boost OJT benefits in hope of encouraging greater participation.

Past consensus on efforts in aid of veterans does not preclude, however, the need to reexamine the rationale of the efforts. Will these programs continue to be justified, and do they meet the standards of equity?

Assuming a generation of peace and an all-volunteer armed force are achieved, the losses during military service may be pared significantly. During a sustained peace, the government's responsibilities to help veterans in their readjustment to civilian life are not the same as during wartime. However, if a large peacetime force is to be maintained, veterans are likely to insist that they deserve the same benefits as their predecessors in uniform.

As military duty is converted into a vocation, salaries will be raised and fringe benefits increased. These improvements will reduce the argument for economic losses. And as the length of military service increases, veterans' benefits can be converted into military fringe benefits. Housing and education programs, for example, are available at present to servicemen through the VA on the same basis as veterans and could be easily transferred to the military as fringe benefits. Disabled servicemen could receive rehabilitation through a military workmen's compensation program. Separate employment programs for veterans would be superfluous.

One of the most outstanding features of the VA readjustment programs is its use of a highly decentralized delivery system. Many veterans complete applications while still in the military or receive assistance from local veterans' organizations and need not even visit a VA office to qualify for benefits. Few other federal agencies are as successful in reaching their clientele.

Moreover, in the case of the education and training programs, veterans have considerable freedom of choice in selecting the types of programs they wish to use. Counseling is available, but counselors do not have veto power over an education plan. The VA policy of individual freedom has been successful in helping millions of veterans improve their economic lives and to realize career aspirations they otherwise could not have achieved.

The lessons gained from the VA experience are likely to spread to other programs. The VA's approach to administering post-secondary education assistance has been adopted by Congress in the Basic Education Opportunity Grant program. Although the size (not exceeding $1,400) of the annual grant will be determined by a means test, the certification approach will be used when the program becomes operational. Proposals have been made suggesting that the VA delivery models be applied to other social programs. Proponents believe that aside from maximizing individual freedom of choice, the delivery system based on VA experience will mean more efficient administration of the programs.

Bibliography

Aaron, Henry J. *Shelter and Subsidies.* Washington, D.C.: U.S. Government Printing Office, 1972.

Adams, Leonard P. *The Public Employment Service in Transition, 1933–1968.* Ithaca, N.Y.: New York State School of Industrial and Labor Relations, Cornell University, 1969.

Bureau of Labor Statistics, U.S. Department of Labor. *Employment and Earnings.* Washington, D.C.: U.S. Government Printing Office, April 1972.

——————. *Employment and Earnings.* Washington, D.C.: U.S. Government Printing Office, July 1972.

Congressional Quarterly, Inc. "Veterans." *Congress and the Nation, 1945–1964.* Washington, D.C.: Congressional Quarterly, Inc., 1965.

Department of Veterans Benefits, Veterans Administration. *Record and Evaluation of the Vocational Rehabilitation Program for Service-Connected Disabled Veterans.* Washington, D.C.: U.S. Government Printing Office, 1955.

Printed for the use of the House Committee on Veterans' Affairs.

——————. *Veterans Benefits under Current Educational Programs* 24-72-4 and 24-72-6. June 1972.

Eggertsson, Thrainn. *Economic Aspects of Higher Education Taken under the World War II Bill of Rights.* Columbus, Ohio: Research Foundation, Ohio State University, 1972.

Flyer, Eli S. "Profile of DOD First-Term Enlisted Personnel Separating from Active Duty during 1970" in "Manpower Research Note." Washington, D.C.: Office of the Assistant Secretary of Defense, October 1971. Mimeographed.

Harris, Louis, and Associates, Inc. *A Study of the Problems Facing Vietnam Era Veterans on Their Readjustment to Civilian Life.* Washington, D.C.: U.S. Government Printing Office, 1972.
    Printed for the use of the Senate Committee on Veterans' Affairs, 92d Cong., 2d Sess.

House Committee on Veterans' Affairs. "Veterans Administration Drug Dependence Program." Washington, D.C.: U.S. Government Printing Office, June 1972.

House Subcommittee on Education and Training, Committee on Veterans' Affairs, 92d Cong., 1st Sess. "Hearings on Education and Training Programs Administered by the Veterans Administration" (November 30, 1971). Washington, D.C.: U.S. Government Printing Office, 1972.

House Subcommittee on HUD-Space-Science-Veterans, Committee on Appropriations, 92d Cong., 2d Sess. "Hearings on HUD-Space-Science-Veterans Appropriations for 1973." Washington, D.C.: U.S. Government Printing Office, 1972.

Hoyt, Kenneth B. "Career Education and Career Choice: Implications for the VA." February 8, 1972.
    Address to the National Task Force on Education and the Vietnam Era Veteran, Veterans Administration.

Human Resources Research Organization. "DOD Post-Service Analysis of Men Separating 1 July 1968–31 December 1970." Unpublished data.

Labor-Management Services Administration, U.S. Department of Labor. *Veterans' Reemployment Rights Handbook.* Washington, D.C.: U.S. Government Printing Office, 1970.

Manpower Administration, U.S. Department of Labor. "Establishment of Absolute Preference for Enrollment for Vietnam Veterans in Manpower Training." March 21, 1972. Mimeographed.

————. *The National Apprenticeship Program.* Washington, D.C.: U.S. Government Printing Office, 1968.

Manpower Report of the President, 1971. Washington, D.C.: U.S. Government Printing Office, 1971.

————, *1972*. Washington, D.C.: U.S. Government Printing Office, 1972.

Mussendon, William S., editor. *The Homeowner's Guide*. Washington, D.C.: The Homeowner's Guide, Inc., 1971.

National Advisory Council on Vocational Education. *Employment Problems of the Vietnam Veteran*. Washington, D.C.: National Advisory Council on Vocational Education, February 1, 1972.

President's Commision on Veterans' Pensions. *The Historical Development of Veterans' Benefits in the United States*. Washington, D.C.: U.S. Government Printing Office, 1956.
Report to the House Committee on Veterans' Affairs, 84th Cong., 2d Sess.

Reports and Statistics Service, Veterans Administration. *Data on Vietnam Era Veterans*. Reports and Statistics Service, June 1972.

Richardson, Robert B. *An Examination of the Transferability of Certain Military Skills and Experience to Civilian Occupations, Final Report*. September 1967.
Prepared for the Office of Manpower Policy, Evaluation and Research, U.S. Department of Labor.

Senate Subcommittee on Health and Hospitals, Committee on Veterans' Affairs, and Subcommittee on Alcoholism and Narcotics, Committee on Labor and Public Welfare, 92d Cong., 1st Sess. "Hearings on Drug Addiction and Abuse among Military Veterans" (June 23, 1971). Washington, D.C.: U.S. Government Printing Office, 1971.

Senate Subcommittee on Veterans' Affairs, Committee on Labor and Public Welfare, 92d Cong., 2d Sess. "Hearings on Unemployment and Overall Readjustment Problems of Returning Veterans" (December 3, 1970). Washington, D.C.: U.S. Government Printing Office, 1971.

U.S. Bureau of the Census. "The Social and Economic Status of Negroes in the United States, 1970." *Current Population Reports*. Washington, D.C.: U.S. Government Printing Office, July 1971.

————. *Statistical Abstract of the United States, 1971*. Washington, D.C.: U.S. Government Printing Office, 1971.

————. *Statistical Abstract of the United States, 1972*. Washington, D.C.: U.S. Government Printing Office, 1972.

U.S. Department of Defense. "Transition Program." March 20, 1972. Mimeographed.

U.S. Department of Labor. "Listing of Job Vacancies with the Federal-State Employment System." *Federal Register* XXXVI: 178–71.

U.S. General Accounting Office. *Drug Abuse Control Program Activities in Vietnam* B-164031(2).

————. *Drug Abuse Control Activities Affecting Military Personnel* B-164031(2).

————. *Most Veterans Not Completing Correspondence Courses* B-114859–72.

Veterans Administration. *Correspondence Courses in Schools below College Level (Cumulative through 1971).* Mimeographed.

————. "Programs of the Study of Peacetime Disabled Veterans, January 1963 through November 30, 1970." Mimeographed.

————. "Rehabilitation Rates: Vocational Rehabilitation Trainees." Unpublished material.

————. *Schools below the College Level (Cumulative from June 1, 1966, through June 30, 1971).* Mimeographed.

————. *Two Years of Outreach, 1968–1970.* Washington, D.C.: U.S. Government Printing Office, 1970.

Veterans Employment Service, U.S. Department of Labor. "Review and Analysis Report: The President's Veterans Program." March 31, 1972. Mimeographed.

Waldman, Elizabeth. "Viet Nam War Veterans: Transition to Civilian Life." *Monthly Labor Review,* November 1970.

————, and Gover, Kathryn R. "Employment Situation of Vietnam Era Veterans." *Monthly Labor Review,* September 1971.

Weinstein, Paul A. *Labor Market Activity of Veterans: Some Aspects of Military Spillover, Final Report.* August 1967.
Prepared for the Office of Education, U.S. Department of Health, Education and Welfare.

Wright, Don D. "Vietnam Veterans: Odd Men Out Move Back to Seattle." *Opportunity,* July 1972.

Index